ideas number seventeen
ideas number eighteen
ideas number nineteen
ideas number twenty

Four Complete Volumes of Ideas in One

Edited by Wayne Rice and Mike Yaconelli.
Previously published as four separate books.

ISBN 0-910125-29-5 (Ideas Combo 17-20)
ISBN 0-910125-00-7 (Ideas Library)
© 1976, 1977, 1981 by Youth Specialties
1224 Greenfield Drive, El Cajon, CA 92021
619/440-2333

Ideas in this book have been voluntarily submitted by individuals
and groups who claim to have used them in one form or another
with their youth groups. Before you use an idea, evaluate it for
its suitability to your own groups, for any potential risks, for
safety precautions that must be taken, and for advance
preparation that may be required. Youth Specialties, Inc., is not
responsible for, nor has it any control over, the use or misuse of
any of the ideas published in this book.

table of contents

CHAPTER FOUR: SPECIAL EVENTS 156

CHAPTER FIVE: SKITS 168

CHAPTER SIX: CAMPING 184

CHAPTER SEVEN: SERVICE PROJECTS 190

CHAPTER EIGHT: PUBLICITY & PROMOTION 197

CHAPTER NINE: THE FAMILY 199

There are lots more ideas where these came from.

This book is only one of an entire library of **Ideas** volumes that are available from Youth Specialties. Each volume is completely different and contains tons of tried and tested programming ideas submitted by the world's most creative youth workers. Order the others by using the form below.

Combo Books

52 volumes of **Ideas** have been updated and republished in four-volume combinations. For example, our combo book **Ideas 1-4** is actually four books in one—volumes 1 through 4. These combos are a bargain at $19.95 each (that's 50% off!).

The Entire Library

The **Ideas** library includes every volume and an index to volumes 1-52. See the form below for the current price, or call the Youth Specialties Order Center at 800/776-8008.

SAVE UP TO 50%!

Your Idea May Be Worth $100

It's worth at least $25 if we publish it in a future volume of **Ideas**. And it's worth $100 if it's chosen as the outstanding idea of the book it appears in.

It's not really a contest, though—just our way of saying thanks for sharing your creativity with us. If you have a good idea that worked well with your group, send it in. We'll look it over and decide whether or not we can include it in a future **Ideas** book. If we do, we'll send you at least 25 bucks!

In addition to that, the **Ideas** editor will select one especially creative idea from each new book as the outstanding idea of that particular book—and send a check for $100 to its contributor.

So don't let your good ideas go to waste. Write them down and send them to us, accompanied by this form. Explain your ideas completely (without getting ridiculous) and include illustrations, diagrams, photos, samples, or any other materials you think are helpful.

FILL OUT BELOW

Name _____

Address_____

City _____ State ___ Zip _____

Phone (_____) _____

I hereby submit the attached idea(s) to Youth Specialties for publication in **Ideas** and guarantee that, to my knowledge, the publication of these ideas by Youth Specialties does not violate any copyright belonging to another party. I understand that, if accepted for publication in **Ideas**, the idea(s) becomes property of Youth Specialties. I understand that I will receive payment for these ideas, the exact amount to be determined by Youth Specialties, payable upon acceptance.

Signature _____

Write or type your idea(s) (one idea per sheet) and attach it to this form or to a copy of this form. Include your name and address with each idea you send. Mail to Ideas, 1224 Greenfield Drive, El Cajon, CA 92021. Ideas submitted to Youth Specialties cannot be returned.

Chapter One

Crowd Breakers

BAGPIPES

This really can't be called a song, but it is fun enough not to matter. Divide your group into three sections. The first section sings "Oh" continuously while lightly hitting their Adam's apples with the side of their hands. The second group sings "Ah" and rhythmically pinches their noses giving both a straight and nasal tone. The third group holds their noses and to the tune of "The Campbells Are Coming" sings using the "da" sound. Done correctly, this really does sound like bagpipes, provided the kids can keep from laughing. (Contributed by Marge Clark, Cocoa, Florida)

BLACKLIGHT BODY PAINTING

Bring a "blacklight" and some fluorescent paint (water soluble) in lots of wild colors to your meeting. As kids come in, start painting their faces with words, symbols, lines, figures, etc. Some won't dig it at first, but after they see everybody else getting into it, they will too. After everybody is painted, turn out the lights and turn on the blacklight. It really looks wild and kids love it. You can then go ahead with some singing or activity this way. (Contributed by Ron Wilburn, El Paso, Texas)

CAREER GUESS

If you are planning a "careers" night with your youth group, try this as an ice breaker. Put up a large sheet of newsprint or paper for each person present if you don't have enough wall space, tape the sheets to the tops of tables). Write each person's name at the top of one sheet and then give everybody a magic marker. Each person should go to every sheet except his/her own and write the occupation that he/she thinks that person will or should be in after their education is completed. (Any criteria is ok). After everyone is finished, each person should write his/her own projected career on their sheet. (Contributed by Marja Coons, Albuquerque, New Mexico)

CHRISTMAS CONFUSION

This idea is based on "Confusion" found in *Ideas Number Fourteen,* page five. It is a great crowd breaker for parties or socials.

Simply give everyone in your group a copy of the instructions below. Read over the instructions to the group to make sure they understand them. The object is to finish all the instructions correctly before anyone else. The first one finished can receive a prize of some kind. There is no correct order so the instructions can be completed in whatever order you want.

Christmas Confusion

1. Get five autographs on the back of this sheet (first, middle, last names).

2. Find three other people and sing together, "We Wish You A Merry Christmas" as loudly as you can. Then initial each other's papers here. _____ _____ _____

3. Tell someone the names of three of Santa's reindeer. Then have that person initial here. _____

4. You play Santa Claus. Find someone of the opposite sex, sit him or her on your lap and ask what he or she wants for Christmas. Then have him or her initial here. _____

5. Pick the ornament on the Christmas tree which you like the best. Find someone else and give them a 15 second speech on why you like that particular ornament. Then have that person initial here. _____

6. You are Ebenezer Scrooge. Find someone and ask them to wish you a Merry Christmas. When they do, say, "Bah, Humbug," ten times while jumping up and down. Then have that person initial here. _____

7. Leapfrog over someone wearing red or green. Then have them initial here. _____

8. Find someone of the opposite sex and have them whistle one verse of "Away In A Manger" to you. Then have that person initial here. _____

(Contributed by Mark and Joanne Parson, Worthington, Minnesota)

CORK GAME

Here's a good "get acquainted" game. Have your group sit in a circle with one less chair than there are participants. Each person seated is required to learn the full name of the person seated to his or her left. One person is left in the middle of the circle. The person in the middle then approaches any person seated, points to them, says "left" or "right", and then counts to ten. The person pointed to must give the first and last name of the one on the left or right. If the one pointed to does not give the correct name, a black cork mark is put on their face and they must change places with the one in the middle. If the person pointed to does give the correct name, the person in the middle gets the black mark on their face.

Every once in a while, the leader yells, "switch", and everyone must exchange seats by going to the opposite side of the circle. One person will end up without a seat and receives a black mark. Each person seated , quickly learns the name of the people on either side and the game continues. (Contributed by Charles Paulson, San Luis Obispo, California)

FACE DECORATING

Have several couples participate in this one. Each girl is given items necessary for cake decorating (squeeze tubes of icing, whipped cream, candy sprinkles, etc.) and they decorate their guy partner's face. The boy should lie down on his back. When finished, the guys stand and have their faces judged, either by the audience or a panel of judges. (Contributed by Ben Smith, Enid, Oklahoma)

GETTING TO KNOW YOU

Give everyone in your group a copy of the chart below. Each person attempts to get people to sign a box containing a description that *truthfully* describes them. The first person to get all the boxes signed, or after a reasonable time, the one with the most boxes signed wins. People can sign more than one box if the description truthfully describes them.

The winner as described above, then reads back to the group the signers and the description they signed under. It creates a lot of laughs. (Adapted from an idea contributed by David Bransby, Sepulveda, California)

(Chart on next page.)

I feel like my breath is bad.	I am madly in love with someone in this room.	On a scale of ten, my sex appeal is about a 3.	The last date I went on was real bad.
I have dandruff.	I am on a diet.	I am good looking, but not conceited.	I want to be President of the U.S.
I have seriously considered trading my folks in on a new stereo.	Basically, my brother/sister is a turkey.	I am afraid of the dark.	I think school is a waste of time.
I don't like my voice. It's too high.	I have B.O. a lot.	I am going to be famous someday.	All of my teeth are not real.

THE HEN SHE CACKLES

Place three chairs in front of the group (make sure the middle chair is flat). Explain to the group that you want to do an exercise in communication and will need five volunteers. Three to be "mediators" and two people to be "arguers" (both the arguers have been clued in ahead of time). The five people are chosen and two of the mediators are asked to leave the room because this is an exercise to see who has better skills at mediating. The two arguers are placed on the outside seats with the mediator in the middle chair. The mediator is told to say and do everything that the two on either side say and do. (To make it look unrehearsed, also explain to the arguers what they are supposed to say and do).

1st arguer to mediator, "The hen she cackles." (Mediator relays)
2nd arguer to mediator, "What?" (Mediator relays)
1st arguer to mediator, "The hen she cackles." (Mediator relays)
2nd arguer to mediator, "I don't understand." (Mediator relays)
1st arguer to mediators, "like this." (He gets up and puts hands in armpits and makes like a chicken cackling and then sits down.)

When the mediator gets up and starts cackling like a chicken, then one of the two arguers puts an egg on his chair which he promptly sits on. This skit can also be made to backfire on the first arguer by cluing in the mediator to what's going on and handing him an egg. (Contributed by Rick Mally, Chicago, Illinois)

HIDDEN NAME

This idea was used for a Valentine event, but could be used

anywhere. Each person is given a name tag and a sheet of paper containing valentine themed sentences. In each name is hidden the name of someone present at the event.

Please be *gene*rous with your love. (Gene)
I'll be in a *mae*lstrom if you won't be mine. (Mae)
J'aime te, mon cher. (Jaime)
Te a*doro thy* lips, love. (Dorothy)

As soon as a person deciphers the name out of the sentence, they are to get the signature of the person belonging to that name. The names are spelled correctly but sometimes a word in a sentence must be misspelled to fit in the more difficult names: I've been in a ne*beulah*ous state since I met you (Beulah). The one getting the most signatures receives a prize. (Contributed by Rowena Lee, Apple Valley, California)

IDENTITY

As your group enters the room, have them fill out a name tag and drop it in a basket. After everyone has arrived, have them stand in a circle. Pass the basket around and have each person take a name tag (not their name) without letting everyone else see the name.

Then have everyone turn to the left and place the name tag they are holding on the back of the person standing in front of them. The object of the game is to discover the name printed on the name tag pinned to their back. They find out their identity by asking questions that can be answered "yes" or "no." Questions like, "Do I have red hair?" or "Am I wearing jeans?". Each kid can only ask two questions of each person they meet.

When a person discovers whose name they have, they then go to that person, place their hands on his/her shoulders and proceed to follow them around the room. As more people discover their identity, the lines of people with hands on shoulders will lengthen until the last person finds their identity. (Contributed by Craig Naylor, Tampa, Florida)

KISS OFF

Bring three guys to the front of the room. Select a girl partner for each one (preferably their dates, if they have any). Tell each guy that they will be blindfolded and kissed by each of the three girls. They are then to determine which girl kisses the best. Of course, if dates are used, each guy will be under a lot of pressure to guess his own girl friend's kiss.

After the guys are blindfolded, you secretly bring in each guy's mother. (This has to be arranged ahead of time, obviously.) "Girl

11

Number One" is first asked to kiss each boy. But little do the boys know that they are going to be kissed by their mothers, not by the girls. Girl Number Two is asked to kiss each boy, and the same thing happens. Each mother kisses her own son, only a little differently this time. After the third kiss, each boy chooses the best kisser, and then all three are allowed to remove their blindfolds. The results can be very interesting. (Contributed by Nathan Daniel, Waco, Texas)

LET ME INTRODUCE MYSELF

Here's a crowd breaker idea for youth who know each other somewhat. Have each person write a short paragraph on themselves using the pronoun "I." Tell them to be somewhat vague and to try and hide their identity, but to be truthful. Hand the paragraphs to a "reader" who will then read the paragraphs and allow the others in the group to discuss the paragraph and then guess the writer's identity. Of course, the person who wrote the paragraph will have to remain elusive during the discussion. The object is to try and fool the group, which encourages kids to share things about themselves not already known. This works best with a group of about ten. (Contributed by George E. Gaffga, Liberty Corner, New Jersey)

LOVELY CONFUSION

Here's a Valentine's Day version of "Confusion" (see Ideas #14). Give everyone the list as printed below. Each person is on his/her own and the first person to accomplish all ten instructions is the winner. (They do not have to be accomplished in order, but they must all be done.)

1. Get ten different autographs. First, middle and last names. (On the back of this sheet)

2. Unlace someone's shoe, lace it and tie it again.

3. Find two other people and the three of you form a heart shape lying on the floor.

4. Get a girl to kiss this paper five (5) times and sign her name. _____

5. If a girl — have a boy get down on his knee and propose to you. If you are a boy — get down on your knee and propose to any girl. Sign his/her name _____

6. Eat ten (10) red hots and show your red tongue to someone you do not know well. They sign here _____

7. Say this poem as loudly as you can.

> How do I love thee
> Let me count the ways
> I love thee to the depth and
> Breadth and height my soul can reach.
> I love thee to the level of every day's most
> quiet need,
> I love thee with the breath, smiles, tears of
> All my life
> And if God choose I shall but love thee
> Better after death.

8. Ask ten (10) people to be your valentine and record your score.

   Yes _____ No _____

9. Leap frog over someone five (5) times.

10. You were given a piece of buble gum at the beginning of the race. Chew it up and blow five (5) bubbles. Find someone who will watch you do it and sign here when you finish.

(Contributed by Joe Snow, Midwest City, Oklahoma)

MATCH UP

Here's a good game that can be used as a crowd breaker or mixer. It really gets people talking and mixing with each other, and it's a lot of fun. Index cards are typed or written with statements like those listed below. The words in italics are typed onto the small right-hand portion of the card, which is then cut off (see illustration).

A SAMPLE LIST OF PHRASES:
I always eat bacon with *my eggs.*
Tarzan lived in the jungle with his wife *Jane.*
The worth of the American dollar is about *40 cents.*
We could save on gasoline with fewer *"jackrabbit starts."*
To get a mule's attention you must first hit him with *a board.*
What good is a peanut butter sandwich without *peanut butter?*
Speak softly and carry a big *stick.*

The large and small portions of the cards are handed out at random to people with the instructions that they are to find the correct match-up with their portion. They must do this by going up to someone introducing themselves, and then holding their cards together and reading them out loud. Some combinations can be very funny. If two people think they have a match, they must go to the designated leader who has all the correct answers, and check to make sure. If they have a correct match, they can sit down. Another variation is to give everyone a large and small portion of cards (which do not match) and make them find both matches.
(Contributed by Kenneth Richards, Park Ridge, Illinois)

MEET THE PRESS

Here's a great way to help the kids in your group to become better acquainted. First, have the kids "mingle" and try to find out as much as possible about each other that they did not already know. After five minutes or so of this have the group divide up into teams or smaller groups.

One person is then chosen at random to "Meet the Press." The chosen person sits at the front of the room while each team receives some paper and a pencil. Each group must write the chosen person's name on the paper and a list of twenty truthful statements about him or her. Allow another five or ten minutes for this.

When these are completed, they are then collected and read back to the entire group (one at a time) and the team with the most correct statements is declared the winner. The person being described judges the statements as to their truthfulness.

In case of a tie, extra value can be given to statements that are less obvious. For example, "born in Nebraska," or "enjoys Shakespeare" shows more insight than, "has red hair."

This exercise is not only fun, but promotes community and friendliness within the group. You can adapt it in many ways, such as by having everyone make a list rather than in teams (best with smaller groups). You may also have more than one "Meet the Press" person per meeting. (Contributed by Tom Bougher, Grand Junction, Colorado)

NAME SEARCH

The purpose of this is to get people who don't know each other to become familiar with the names of everyone in the group. Make sure there are no lists containing the names of the group anywhere visible; instead, put a large name tag on each person.

```
K  E  U  S  O  L  D  X  N

A  L  L  A  N  A  R  F  V

T  T  O  K  R  S  J  A  D

H  T  E  B  A  Z  I  L  E

Y  R  G  G  L  T  Z  R  Y

R  E  T  E  P  P  L  A  K

M  I  J  K  H  L  R  A  C

T  R  S  H  A  R  O  N  W
```

Give each person a word search puzzle with every person's name somewhere in the puzzle. Of course, to do the puzzle, people have to know the names they are looking for, which means there will be a lot of walking around and looking at name tags. (Contributed by Bruce H. Schlenke, Akron, Ohio)

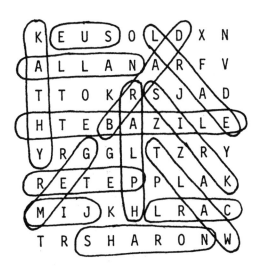

NAME THE NEIGHBORS

Here is a fun problem of logic that might come in handy sometime when you want to keep a group occupied:

Fran, Grace, Helen, Ida, and Jane and their husbands all live on a certain street that runs east to west in the town of Centerville. From the following clues, give each couple's full names and describe exactly where on the street each couple lives.

1. Grace has Ralph as one next door neighbor and the Greens as her other next door neighbor.
2. The Browns live in the westernmost house - Ned in the easternmost.
3. Sam has Ida as one next door neighbor and Peter as his next door neighbor on the other side.
4. Both Jane and Peter live east of the Whites.
5. Peter lives next door to the Blacks.
6. Tom lives west of the Greys, and east of Grace.
7. Helen and Jane are next door neighbors. The Greys live next to Jane also, but on the other side.

Solution (from west to east on the street)

(Contributed by Angus Emerson, Little Rock, Arkansas)

PASTOR SPLICE

First of all, obtain reel to reel tapes of several of your pastor's sermons. With the help of two tape recorders, splicing equipment, and electrically inclined helpers, splice and edit phrases of the pastor's sermons as answers to your own contrived questions. You can then play an authentic interview with the pastor with some rather hilarious results. Here is a sample from one such interview.

Int: Describe your boy, Peter, in two words.
Pas: Behavioural problem.
Int: How about your other son, Dave?
Pas: Lazy and weak.

(Contributed by Rick Porter, Omaha, Nebraska)

QUEEN ANNE'S RIDDLE

This is one of those "Brain teaser" games that is fun at informal get-togethers when there's nothing else to do. The object is to solve the riddle. One person (who knows the answer) starts by giving the first part of the riddle: "It is a queen, but not a king." As soon as a person knows what the secret is, they show this by adding to the riddle, rather than giving away the answer. This keeps the game going until everyone "gets it" or falls asleep, whichever comes first. The riddle might go something like this:

"It is a queen, not a king...yellow but not blue...green but not red...a roof but not a ceiling...a door but not a window... Jimmy but not James...a wheel but not a tire...the moon but not the sun...."

"It" is any word with a double letter. (Contributed by John F. Brug, West Newton, Pennsylvania)

S AND T

Divide the group down the middle. Have one side be the "S and T's" and the other side be the "Everything Else's." The idea is that you will count together as a group from one to twenty, and every time you say a number that begins with an "S" or a "T," the "S and T" group stands up. On all the other numbers, the "Everything Else" group stands up. Start slow, then do it again a little faster. Each time the "Everything Else's" stand on "one," and the "S and T's" stand on "two and three," and so on. It really gets wild the faster you go.

To make more of a game out of this, have everyone sit in a circle, and start counting around the circle, "1,2,3, 4, etc." up to 20 and then start at "1" again, and so on. Every time a person says a number that begins with an S or T, they must stand up before saying it. If they don't, they are out of the game, and the game continues. The counting must be done in rhythm without waiting (or you are eliminated). It's very confusing, but lots of fun. (Contributed by Sam Walker, Sheboygan, Wisconsin)

SIGNATURES

This is a mixer that can be used with any age group. It's easy and fun to play. Give each person a sheet of paper and a pencil. Written down the left hand border of the paper are the letters in a word or phrase selected because of its association with the holiday or the occasion of the party. For example, at a Christmas party, the words written down the side might be "Merry Christmas."

On a signal, the players go around getting the signatures of the other players. They try to find someone whose first or last name begins with one of the letters in the key word or phrase. When someone is found, they are asked to sign next to the appropriate letter. The first person to get signatures next to all of the letters on his or her sheet is the winner. If no winner has come forth after a certain period of time, stop the game, and whoever has the most signatures found is the winner. In case of a tie, first names that match are worth more than last names - so the most matching first names wins. For larger groups, the phrase can be longer, or shorter for smaller groups. (Contributed by Lillian Rossow, Sandusky, Ohio)

STATISTICAL TREASURE HUNT

Here is an exceptionally good game at getting groups acquainted. Divide group into teams of equal number, if possible. Give each team a typewritten or mimeographed sheet of questions which are to be answered and evaluated as indicated on the sheet. Each team appoints a captain who acts as the gleaner of information and recorder. The game can be played around tables at banquet events.

Below is a list of typical questions and methods of scoring. You may not want to use all of these. These may suggest other questions to you which may be more appropriate for your particular group or occasion.

General Questions:

_____1. Counting January as one point, February as two points and so on through the calendar year, add up the total of birthday points at your table. Just ask 'em what month they were born, not the year!

_____2. Counting one point for each different state named, give score for different number of birth states represented on your team.

_____3. Total of all shoe sizes added together. One foot only.

_____4. Total number of operations everyone at your table has had. Serious dental surgery counts, but not just an ordinary tooth pulling. You must have time to count the number, no time for all the interesting details!

_____5. Get your hair color score: Black counts two; brown counts one; blonde counts three; red counts five; gray counts three; white counts five.

_____6. Score a point for each self-made article worn or carried by your teammates.

_____7. Add the total number of miles traveled by each member to get to this meeting.

_____8. Total number of children teammates have. If husbands and wives are sitting together or are on one team, count their children only once. Score as follows: Each child counts one point; set of twins counts five points; grandchildren count three points each.

_____9. Score one point for each different college attended, but not necessarily graduated from.

(Contributed by Angus Emerson, Little Rock, Arkansas)

STICKER MIXER

Here's a good get-acquainted activity for larger groups. Write everyone's name on a sticker (pressure-sensitive - round ones work best) and distribute them at random. Have everyone stick the label on their face somewhere. Then everyone tries to find their own name on someone else's face. When a person finds their name, they get the sticker and stick it on their shirt or coat and stay with the person on whom they found their name until he or she finds their name. This is a good way for kids to see a lot of faces in a short time. (Contributed by Don Rubendall, Muncie, Indiana)

STRING TIE MYSTERY

Here's a simple little game that you can use to test your group's creativity. Hang two strings from the ceiling in such a way that they dangle approximately one foot from the floor (both strings should be about the same length). The strings should be far enough apart that, while holding the dangling end of one string, the other string hanging down is a foot or so out of reach. Challenge anyone in your group to tie the dangling ends of the strings together with no help from the audience. The only thing that can be used in this task is an ordinary pair of plyers.

How is it done? Simple. Tie the plyers to the end of one of the strings and then swing the string back and forth. Then hold the end of the other string, and when the plyers swing close enough, grab them. Untie the plyers and tie the two strings together. (Contributed by Dennis Banks, St. Petersburg, Florida)

TEN YEARS FROM NOW

This is a good way for kids to get to know each other better. Divide into groups of eight to ten. Have each person pick someone in their group they know the least and have them go off into some private corner and ask each other questions such as:

1. How has your personality changed (if any) in the last five years?
2. What are some of the things that you really like to do?
3. What are some of the things that you don't like to do?

4. Do you have any hobbies? Name them if you do.
5. Tell about an embarrassing situation from your past.
6. Name something you are pretty good at.
7. In what type of situation are you the most comfortable? Uncomfortable?
8. What are your favorite classes at school? Least favorite?
9. What has been bugging you the most lately?
10. Do you have any "heroes" - people you really admire?

Once everyone is finished, have them assemble into their groups and then ask each person to think about the person they interviewed and try to make a prediction about them, such as "Ten years from now, _____ will be..." Have them share their predictions with the rest of the group. (Contributed by Bob Gleason, Winchester, Oregon)

UP AND DOWN BONNIE

Here's a great variation to the song, "My Bonnie Lies Over The Ocean." While singing the song, have everyone stand on the first word that begins with a "B" and sit down on the next word that begins with "B." Continue the same process on all the "B" words. For variation, have half the group start the song standing up. People get confused about whether they are to be standing or sitting. Lots of fun. (Contributed by Darrell Simpkins, Camden, South Carolina)

WHAT'S THE MEANING?

Here is a good quiz that can be used for fun at parties, socials, or to keep kids busy on a long bus trip. Each of the following combinations of letters or numbers represents a well-known saying or tells a story. The object is to decipher each one.

GIRL FELLOW FELLOW	11
L E G A L	EZ
GIRL $1,000,000	ll
FAR HOME	YOUR HAT
GNIKOOL	KEEP IT
<u>MONEY</u>	
SUN., MON., TUES.,	
THURS., FRI., SAT.	
RRRRRRR	
RRRRRRR	
RRRRRRR	
RRRRRRR	
RRRRRRR	
RRRRRRR	
RRRRRRR	

```
                    G
                   N
                  I
                H
               T
              Y
             R
            E
           V
          E
        WETHER
```

```
A L L O                          WORL

2th DK                           BANGFF

   0                             BRILLIANT SURGEON
                                 BRILLIANT SURGEON
D.D.S.
LL.D                             N
PH.D                               E
M.A.                                 W
M.D.                             THINGS

O U T                            WOWOLFOL
3 2 1
                                 SSSSSSSSSS C
RE  RE
                                  S   H   I   P
EVERY RIGHT THING

F FAR E FAR W
```

The answers (in order of appearance):

Two fellows after the same girl	One after another
Legal separation	Easy on the eyes
Girl with a million-dollar figure	Keep it under your hat
Far away from home	Everythings going up
Looking backwards	Bad spell of weather
Money on the line	
A week with one day off	
Forty-niners	World without end
	Starting off with a bang
	A couple of sharp operators
Nothing after all	A new slant on things
Tooth decay	Wolf in sheep's clothing
Five degrees below zero	Tennessee
Outnumbered three to one	Space ship
Repaired	
Right between everything	
Few and far between	

(Contributed by Angus Emerson, Little Rock, Arkansas)

WHOPPER

This is an interesting activity for groups that know each other fairly well. Give each person the questionnaire below. Instruct them to tell the truth in answer to four of the questions, but to lie in response to one of the questions. The "whopper" should sound reasonable. After everyone is finished, each person then reads their answers to the rest of the group and they try to guess which answer is the "whopper."

Answer each of the five questions below. Tell the truth on four of them and tell a "whopper" on one.

1. Where were you born?

2. How many siblings (brothers and sisters, dummy) do you have?

3. What are your hobbies?

4. Where were you at 10:00 last Saturday night?

5. What do you hope to have as a career?

(Contributed by Don Klompeen, San Francisco, California)

Chapter Two

Games

AUNT SALLY

This game is not only fun to play but entertaining to watch. Line up six to eight chairs side by side. Choose five kids to sit in the chairs with the leader on the end. The leader starts by saying, "Aunt Sally went to town." The person next to the leader replies, "Really? What did she buy?" The leader responds, "Some knitting needles." (Makes motions of knitting). The dialogue and actions are repeated until the last one in line repeats the dialogue to the leader. While everyone is making the motions of knitting, the leader begins the dialogue again, "Aunt Sally went to town". The person next to the leader responds, "Really? What did she buy?" The leader replies, "A rocking chair". (Begins rocking on chair while still knitting) Continue down the line again. This game can continue as long as you can think of things that Aunt Sally buys. Here are some suggestions:

> Stand up machine (stand up and down)
> Hula-hoop (pantomime hula-hooping)
> Bicycle (jump up and pedal in the air)

After you have enough actions you can end with "Aunt Sally went to town". "Really? What did she buy?" "Nothing, she died." (Contributed by Bo McKinney, Rockwall, Texas)

BACK BALL RELAY

This game can be played indoors or out-of-doors. Divide the group into teams of six or more on a team. Then each team has its members pair up. The first couple from each team stands behind the starting line. A ball (basketball or a volleyball) is then placed between them just above the belt line as the couple stands back to back. The object of the relay is, with their arms folded in front of them and not using their elbows, to carry the ball around a chair (about 30 feet away) and back again without dropping it. If the ball is dropped the couple must start over. When the couple successfully complete their round trip, the next couple places the ball between their backs and does the same thing. The first team to have all of its couples successfully complete the relay are the winners. If a team does not have an even number, someone can go twice. The couples do not need to be of the opposite sex.

This is more difficult than it may sound. The couple must really communicate and work together or else they will drop the ball and start over any number of times. If a couple cannot do it after several attempts, have them go to the back of the line so that the rest will have a chance to try it. (Contributed by Samuel Hoyt, Lansing, Michigan)

BACK TO BACK

Divide your group into pairs and have them sit on the floor back to back and link arms. Then tell them to stand up. With a little timing and sensitivity, it shouldn't be too hard. Then combine two pairs into a foursome. Have the foursome sit on the floor back to back with arms linked. Tell them to stand up. It is a little harder with four. Keep adding more people to the group until the giant blob can't stand up any more. (Contributed by Marshall Shelley, Elgin, Illinois)

BACK TO BACK RELAY

This is a variation of the old "three legged race." Rather than tying two people side by side, you instead tie two people together back to back. One of them runs forward, and the other runs backward. When they reach the finish line, instead of turning around to run back, the one who ran forwards now runs backwards. Players should be tied together at the waist with a rope or belt. When one pair finishes, the next pair goes. First team to finish is the winner. (Contributed by Burney Heath, Cape Coral, Florida)

BALLOON BLOWER BASKETBALL

Have one team line up behind the free throw line at one end of the basketball court and one team at the other end. Each team designates someone as their "balloon blower." At the signal, the first person in line shoots a basketball from the free throw line or dribbles as close as they want to the net and shoots. The second person in line must stay behind the free throw line until the ball is thrown back to them by the person who just shot. After a person shoots, they get back in line. Each time someone makes a basket, the "balloon blower" makes one giant blow into the balloon. The team which pops their balloon first wins. If you want the game to go longer, you can give each team two or three balloons. (Contributed by Jon Hantsbarger, Carthage, Missouri)

BALLOON KITE WAR

Here's a great idea for a sunny afternoon at the park, church picnic, or part of a larger special event. Have your kids bring a kite and a needle to a pre-determined area. Don't tell them what is going to happen. Make sure the place you meet is a large open area.

Put aloft several large weather balloons, or large regular balloons filled with helium and attached to strong cords. The first person to launch their kite armed with a needle (be sure to bring masking tape) and pop the balloon up in the air, wins. (Contributed by Dick Baugh

BEACH BALL PICKUP

Divide into teams. Teams then number off and line up opposite each other about twenty feet or so apart. Between the two teams, six beach balls (light ones) are placed on the floor. Two numbers are called and the two players on each team with those numbers begin play. Each couple must pick up three balls without using their hands or arms. If they drop a ball, they must start over. All three balls must be held between the two players and must be off the ground. The first couple to succeed is the winner. Repeat by calling two new numbers, and so on. (Contributed by Dave Gilliam, Grove, Oklahoma)

BEDLAM

This game requires four teams of equal size. Each team takes one corner of the room or playing field. The play area can be either square or rectangular. On a signal (whistle, etc.), each team attempts to move as quickly as possible to the corner directly across from their corner (diagonally) performing an announced activity as they go. The first team to get all its members into its new corner wins that particular round. The first round can be simply running to the opposite corner, but after that you can use any number of possibilities: walking backward, wheelbarrow racing (one person is the wheelbarrow), piggyback, rolling somersaults, hopping on one foot, skipping, "crab walking", etc. There will be literally mass bedlam in the center as all four teams crisscross. (Contributed by Norma Bailey, Colora, Maryland)

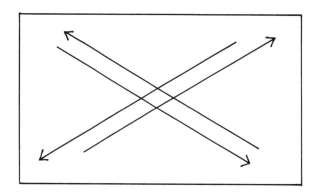

BIG BOPPER

This exciting game is similar to frozen tag. Instead of the one who is "it" tagging people, "it" (called the "bopper") bops people with a "bataca bat,", rolled-up newspaper or similar object. When someone is "bopped" they must not only stay frozen, but they must begin making appropriate sounds (such as "ohhh", or "aghhh") that sound like they have been bopped. They must remain frozen and moaning until someone who is free tags them. You can have a safe area for resting. Big Bopper is played best in the dark. (Contributed by Mark Masterson, Ft. Wayne, Indiana)

BIG MOUTH STACK

Here's a game that is great for both individual competition and team relays. The object of the game is to see how high individuals or teams can stack regular alphabet blocks. The only catch is that contestants cannot use anything except their mouth to place the blocks on top of each other.(Contributed by W. Mains, Merrillville, Indiana)

BIRTHDAY BARNYARD

This game is an adaptation of "Barnyard Mixer" (see Ideas #1—4) and would work best with a large group. Give each person a list like the one below. After everyone has received the list they are instructed to look at the action described for the month of their birthday. When the lights are turned out, they are to immediately stand up and make the appropriate action. As soon as they find a person doing the same thing, they lock arms and look for the rest of the team. As soon as all the team is together, they are to sit down. The first team to find all its members wins.

January — Shout "Happy New Year"!
February — Say "Be My Valentine"
March — Blow (wind)
April — Hop (Easter Bunny)
May — say "Mother, May I?"
June — say "Will you marry me?"
July — Make fireworks sounds
August — Sing "Take me out to the ball game"
September — Fall down (fall)
October — shout "Boo!"
November — say "Gobble-Gobble"
December — say "Ho Ho Ho, Merrrry Christmas"

BLIND VOLLEYBALL

Divide the kids into two equal groups. The two teams then get on each side of a volleyball court and sit down either on chairs or on the floor in rows, like in regular volleyball. The "net" should be a solid divider that obstructs the view of the other team, such as blankets hung over a regular volleyball net or rope. The divider should also be low enough that players cannot see under it. Then play volleyball. Use a big, light plastic ball instead of a volleyball. Regular volleyball rules and boundaries apply. A player cannot stand up to hit the ball. The added dimension of the solid net adds a real surprise element to the game when the ball comes flying over the net. (Contributed by John Vincent, Minneapolis, Minnesota)

BLOW CUP RELAY

Give each team a fifteen foot piece of string with a sliding paper cup on the string (see illustration).

The string is held taut and the paper cup is placed at one end and the team lines up single file. At the signal, each player must blow the cup to the other end (with hands behind his/her back) and then

push it back to the start for the next player. The first team to finish wins. (Contributed by Gail Beauchamp, Moorestown, New Jersey)

BROOM WHIRL RELAY

All teams line up in a straight line and the first person of each team is given a broom. The first and the second person hold on to the broom with both hands. On start the pair must turn around in place, so that they start face to face, then go side to side, back to back, side to side, then face to face. Both individuals must hold on to the broom at all times. Then the second and third person repeat what the first and second person did, and so on until the broom reaches the last person. The last person must then run to the front of the line, with the broom, and repeat the process with the first person. The team to do this first wins. One variation is to have each pair turn around 10 times before going to the next person. (Contributed by Bill Flanders, El Toro, California)

BUMBERSHOOT RELAY

Divide your group into two teams. Each team then gets an overcoat, umbrella, and hat (the sillier the better). On the signal, the first person in line puts on the hat and overcoat, opens the umbrella over their head and shouts, "It looks like rain." They pass the items on to the next person who does the same thing. First group through wins. For those too superstitious to open up an umbrella inside, have them put the tip of the umbrella on the floor, and while holding the handle, dance in a circle around the umbrella singing, "I'm singing in the rain." (Contributed by Grady Roe, Austin, Texas)

CATASTROPHE

This game can be used with a group of 15 or more people. Divide the group into three teams, and have each team sit in chairs in three lines, parallel to each other and with about three feet between the teams. All players should be facing the same direction, which is toward the front of their team's line. (Each player sits facing a team-mate's back.)

Each team has the name of a town, such as "Pottstown," "Muds-ville," and "Dry Gulch" (any name will do.) Each player on each team is assigned an "occupation," such as plumber, carpenter, policeman, preacher, teacher, doctor, etc. There should be the same occupations on each team, and they should be seated in the same order on each team as well.

● plumber ● ●
● carpenter ● ●
● preacher ● ●
● policeman ● ●
● teacher ● ●
● doctor ● ●
● mechanic ● ●
● fireman ● ●
Pottstown   Dry Gulch   Mudsville

The leader then calls out an occupation and a town, such as, "We need a policeman at Pottstown." At that point, the policemen on each team must get up out of their chairs, run around their team and return to their chairs. The first person back in his or her chair wins a point for his or her team.

An additional twist to this game is that players must run around their teams in the right direction. This is determined by which town is called. For example, if the team lines are arranged so that Potts-town is on everyone's left, Mudsville is on the right, and Dry Gulch is in the middle, then if Mudsville is called, everyone must get out of their chairs on the right, and run around the team in a clockwise (right) direction. Pottstown would be left, and if Dry Gulch is called, either direction is okay. If you don't run in the correct direction, you lose.

If the leader calls out, "There's been a catastrophe in (town).", then everyone on all three teams must get up and run around the team, again in the correct direction. The first team completely seated gets the point. Remember that everyone must get up from their chairs on the correct side, as well as going around in the right direction. (Contributed by Scott Herrington, Odessa, Texas)

CATCH THE WIND

Have one person lie on the floor with a straw in his mouth. At his head, place a chair. A second person sits in the chair facing the person on the floor and has a party blower in his mouth. The chair back should be towards the person on the floor and the seated person should rest his chin on the chair back. A third person sits next to the person on the floor and places Kleenex (or any other brand) tissues

one at a time on the end of the straw. The person on the floor then blows the tissue up in the air and the person in the chair tries to catch it with the party blower. This game requires three-person teams, obviously, and the winning team is the first to successfully catch a given number of tissues. The distance from the blower on the floor to the catcher may vary depending on the distance up that people can blow. (Contributed by Dave Gilliam, Grove, Oklahoma)

CHAIN REACTION ROCK

Two teams of equal number sit in straight lines facing each other with about five feet between the two teams. (See diagram.) Integrate the sexes as much as possible and have the separate teams hold hands. The leader positions himself at the front of both lines and a medium-sized rock is placed at the end of the two lines equidistant from the end players. Instruct all the players to look at the rock except the front person of each team. The leader flips a coin

and reveals it to the first players simultaneously. If the coin turns up "tails", both teams do nothing, but if it turns up "heads", the front players squeeze the hand of the person beside them, and so on down the line, until the end person feels his or her hand squeezed. The end person then immediately grabs for the rock and the team that grabs the rock first rotates so that the end player is now the first player. The team that rotates one full revolution of players is the winner. Silence is a must while the coin is being flipped because some kids might squeeze accidently and no warning must be given. If the rock is picked up at any time other than after a "heads" was flipped, the team that picked up the rock rotates in reverse. (Contributed by John Bohling, Anacortes, Washington)

CHOCOLATE SCRAMBLE

Here is a great game for groups of six to ten. Place a chocolate bar in the center of a table. (The candy is still in its wrapper and to make the game last longer, you can wrap the candy in gift wrap paper too.) Each person sitting around the table takes a turn at rolling the die. The first person who rolls a six gets to start eating the candy bar - ONLY after they put on a pair of mittens, cap, scarf; and ONLY after they run once around the table; and ONLY with a knife and fork.

While the person who rolled the six is getting ready (per the instructions above) to eat the candy bar, the group keeps taking turns rolling the die. If someone rolls a six, then the person who rolled the six before them relinquishes their right to the candy bar, and the second person must try to eat the candy before someone else rolls a six. The game is over when all the candy bar is devoured or when everyone drops to the floor with exhaustion. (Contributed by Bob McCormick, Crestline, Ohio)

CIRCLE BOWLING

Place as many bowling pins (or twelve inch long 2 x 4's) as there are couples in a circle. Then have the couples hold hands and form a circle around the "pins". At the signal each person in a couple attempts to pull their partner into a pin and knock it down. Whoever hits a pin is eliminated, new pairs are formed, the appropriate number of pins reset, and a new round begins until a winner emerges. (Contributed by Fred Winslow, Allen, Texas)

CLOTHES PINNING

Here's a wild game that is simple, yet fun to play with any size group. Give everyone in the group six clothespins. On "go," each player tries to pin their clothespins on other players' clothing. Each of your six pins must be hung on six different players. You must keep moving to avoid having clothespins hung on you, yet you try to hang your pins on someone else. When you hang all six of your clothespins, you remain in the game, but try to avoid having more pins hung on you. At the end of a time limit, the person with the least amount of clothespins hanging on him (or her) is the winner and the person with the most is the loser.

Another way to play this is to divide the group into pairs and give each person six clothespins. Each person then tries to hang all their pins on their partner. The winners then pair off again, and so on until there is a champion clothespinner. (Contributed by Prudence Elliott, Willows, California)

CRAB SOCCER

This game is played just like regular soccer except for two variations - the area of play should be smaller (like an indoor gym) and everyone except the goalies must move "crab-like" (on hands and feet with backs to the ground). Goalies can be on their knees and they are the only ones who can use their hands to control the ball. Because of the reduced mobility of the players, it is best if you assign positions (forward, defense, left, right, etc.) (Contributed by Marshall Shelley, Elgin, Illinois)

DAVID AND GOLIATH SLING THROW

Divide the group into two teams ("David I" and "David II"), with the same number of guys and girls on each team. Each team is given one old nylon stocking (someone has said that hose are for water on the knee) and one whiffle ball to place in the toe of the nylon. One person of the same sex steps forward to the throwing line. Each twirls the nylon with the ball in it over his head or at his side and sees who can throw it the farthest. The winner gets one point for his or her team. The team with the most points wins the contest. You can then repeat this contest for accuracy. Set a "Goliath" (a person, chair, or other object) approximately 30 feet away from the throwing line. The person that comes the closest gets one point for his or her team. If he or she should hit "Goliath" an additional bonus point is awarded to the team. The kids will quickly find out that it took much practice for David to be such a skilled marksman.

Caution: Be sure that the teams are perhaps ten yards to the sides of the throwing line because the slings can go forward, backward, or straight up with amateurs throwing. (Contributed by Samuel Hoyt, Lansing, Michigan)

DOMINO

This is a great game for larger groups that is not only fun to play, but fun to watch as well. It's also easy to play and requires no props. Teams line up in single file lines with teams parallel to each other. There should be the same number of people (exactly) in each line, and everyone should face the same direction, toward the front of the line. On a signal (whistle, etc.), the first person in each line squats, then the next person (behind (behind him) also squats, then the next person and so on all the way down to the end of the team's line. (You cannot squat down until the person immediately in front of you squats first.) The last person in line squats and then quickly stands back up again, and the whole process repeats itself, only in reverse, with each person standing up in succession instead of squatting. (Again, you cannot stand up until the person *behind* you first stands up.) The team which completes this first, with the person at the front of the line standing, is the winner.

The effect of this visually is much like standing "dominoes" up side by side and pushing over the one on the end toward the others. Each domino falls in succession to the end of the line. This game is much like that, only the "dominoes" first go down, then back up again. It works best with at least 25 or so in each line (the more the better). Have the group try it several times for speed.

ELASTIC BAND RELAY

In preparation for this game, cut a strip of inch wide elastic 36 inches long. Overlap one inch and stitch on a sewing machine. The result will be a large elastic circle.

Break group into teams of eight to twelve players. Supply each team with an elastic band. At the starting signal, the first player brings the band over his head and body before passing it on to the next player on the team. The first team to have all the players pass the elastic band over their bodies is the winning team.

Variations may have the players passing the elastic band up from the feet, or couples passing the band over both bodies at once. (Contributed by Prudence Elliott, Willows, California)

FEATHER FOOTBALL

Everyone gets down on their hands and knees. There should be two teams. Goal lines are marked on each end of the room. A feather is placed between the two teams, and the idea is to blow the feather across your team's goal line. Limit this game to about six persons on a team. (Contributed by Randall Newburn, Roseburg, Oregon)

FEATHER RELAY

Divide into teams and give each team a box of small feathers (mallard or duck breast feathers are best and are relatively easy to find. If all else fails, visit a fly-tying shop.) There should be one feather for each member of the team. On a signal, the first person on the team blows (through the air) his feather the length of the room and into a small box. At no time may he touch the feather. He may, on the other hand, blow an opponent's feather in the opposite direction if the opportunity arises. The race continues until the team has all their feathers in the box, one at a time. This race can be doubly exciting if done on hands and knees. (Contributed by Randall Newburn, Roseburg, Oregon)

FEET ON THE ROCKS

Divide your group into two teams. Have each team sit back to back with an approximate five foot space between the chairs. (See diagram.) The captain of each team sits in a separate chair at the end of the team row of chairs.

At the signal, an ice cube is placed under one of the feet of each captain. The captains slide the ice to player Number One on their team. Player Number One must pass it from one foot to the other and then to the next player on the team. This continues until the ice cube is passed by the entire team back to the captain again. The captain is now allowed to stand up and devise a way to carry the ice cube with his or her feet only to the opposite end of the room and put it into a cup (no hands).

If the captain drops the ice cube, he or she can start from where it was dropped, but if the ice cube melts or slips out of reach while the team is passing it, they must start over again. (Contributed by Barry Kolanowski, Greeley, Colorado)

FICTITIOUS

Here's a team game that can be lots of fun. Divide into teams of four. Write a word on the blackboard that no one has ever heard of. Give one team the actual definition and have them make up three phony definitions and write all four definitions down. The other teams then try to guess which definition is correct. Two points are given for a correct first vote and one point for a correct second vote. Each team gets a chance to write their phony definitions to a new word. The team with the most points wins. (Contributed by Doc Henry, Imperial, California)

FLAMINGO VOLLEYBALL

Here's a guys vs. gals game that can really be a lot of fun. Announce to your group a volleyball game between the girls and the guys. After the teams are selected and ready to play, give the guys one additional instruction that you supposedly forgot to mention. The rules are the same as regular volleyball except that when the ball is in play, every guy must hold one ankle. Failure to do so results in a point for the other team. (Contributed by Larry Lawrence, Jonesboro, Georgia)

FLOP CHOP BALLOON POP

For this game (or it can be done as a crowd breaker with only two or three kids participating up front), you will need some balloons, elastic, a meat cleaver, a chopping board, and a pole to tie the elastic to. Inflate the balloon and tie one end of the elastic to the balloon. Tie the other end to a pole or something stable. Stretch elastic as far as it will go. Put a mark for the balloon holder to stand behind. Put the chopping block (table) in the middle of the stretched elastic. One person stands at the chopping block with the meat cleaver. The person holding the balloon lets go of the balloon, and as it zips by the chopper, he must chop downward and try to bust the balloon. If he misses (as they usually do), the holder runs and gets the balloon, takes it back to the mark and tries again.

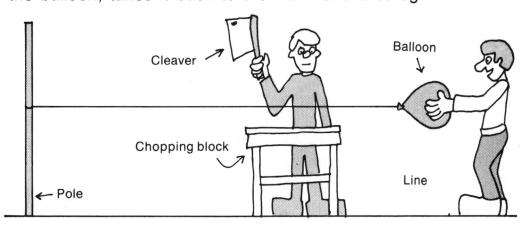

Set a time limit for everyone, and give those who fail to accomplish this task a penalty (the "hot seat" or smack them in the face with a pie). You might have some spare elastic handy for the quick choppers. Only one swing per try is allowed. (Contributed by Dave Gilliam, Grove, Oklahoma)

FOUL SHOOTING MARATHON

If you have access to a basketball court, here's a good game that anybody can play and which allows everyone a chance to get in on the action. You can play with as many teams (at once) as you have baskets, or each team may go one at a time if you only have one basket.

The team lines up at the foul line and the first person in line gets the basketball. On a signal, he or she begins shooting regulation free throws (foul shots), while one teammate stands under the basket and returns the ball as quickly as possible. (The person under the basket can be the person who just finished shooting. That way each person does this job once. Begin with the last person in line.) The shooter continues to shoot until the whistle blows, then he or she becomes the person under the basket, and the next person starts shooting as quickly as possible.

The leader (who is blowing the whistle) may blow the whistle at even 30 second intervals (plus or minus) or may blow it at uneven intervals, giving some players more time than others. The latter is most applicable when all teams are throwing at the same time. That way a player doesn't really know how much time he has to shoot. A scorekeeper should be counting the total number of successful foul shots made, and the team which has the most after everyone has had a chance to throw, wins. To make the game a bit longer, play four "quarters," a quarter being the time it takes for everyone on the team to throw once.

Variations of this game may include these:

1. Two teams can play best out of three rounds, rather than adding the total number of baskets made. In other words, a winner is declared after each round (quarter) and the first team to win two is the champ.

2. You can have each shooter shoot a certain number of shots and then the next person takes over. No whistle is necessary here. Also, the round could be over as soon as one team finishes making all its throws, whether or not the other teams have finished. That way speed enters into the picture.

3. You could also have a shooter shoot until he makes a shot and then move to the next person. If you do it this way, each round

can have a set time limit, say 10 minutes. or, the first team to successfully get one free shot out of each player is the winner of that round.

(Contributed by Norma Bailey, Colora, Maryland)

FOUR TEAM DODGEBALL

This is a fast moving game that is best played in a gym or similar room. Divide the group into four teams of equal size. If you have a basketball court marked on the floor, this can be used as the playing area, otherwise you will need to mark off your own boundaries with tape or some other method. The floor is divided into quadrants similar to the diagram below:

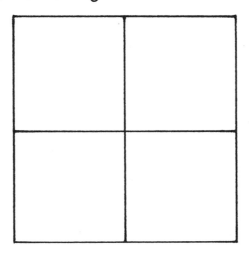

Each team is assigned one of the four areas and team members cannot leave their assigned area during the game. A volleyball, beachball, or playground ball should be used (not as hard or as large as a basketball). The rules are basically the same as regular dodgeball, except that a player may throw the ball at anyone in any of the other three quadrants. If a player is hit below the belt with the ball, he or she is out of the game. If the ball misses and goes out of bounds, the referee tosses the ball into the team that was thrown at (where it went out of bounds). If a player is thrown at and catches the ball before it hits the floor, without dropping it, the player that threw it is out. The winning team is the team that lasts the longest (the team that still has at least one player after the other teams have been eliminated), or the team with the most players left at the end of a specified time limit. (Contributed by Samuel Hoyt, Lansing, Michigan)

FRISBEE RUGBY

Divide your group into two teams (this is played best with twenty five or less players). Set up goals at opposite ends of the field. Team A tries to advance the frisbee over one goal line while Team B tries to advance the frisbee over the opposite goal line. Frisbees can only be advanced by throwing it to a teammate. Each person can only take three steps before throwing the frisbee. If they take more than three steps, frisbee goes to the opposite team. A person must be allowed five seconds to throw the frisbee without harrassment, if they wait longer, they can be "blitzed" by their opponents. If the frisbee is dropped, or if it hits the ground before being caught, the team that had possession last must give it over to the opposing team. (Contributed by Marshall Shelley, Elgin, Illinois)

FRISBEE TOURNAMENT

There are lots of "Frisbee" games in the Ideas Library (FrisBall, Frisbee Golf, Frisbee Relay, etc.), but here's a game event that can involve your youth group for an entire afternoon or evening. Encourage everyone to bring their own frisbees. Bring extras for those who forget and make sure each frisbee is properly identified. Hold the event in a large open area and allow the participants to warm up before the event begins.

SINGLES COMPETITION

1. *Accuracy* — Using a garden hose or rope placed on the ground make a semi-circle around an object, such as a garbage can, at which each participant will throw. Place the object about 15 feet from all points on the semi-circle. All of the competitors throw at the same time. Each person gets two throws at each distance. Those who hit the object from that distance remain in the game; those who miss it after two attempts are out. The object is then moved back three feet and each person left in the competition again gets two chances to hit it once. (If the group is small they can throw individually rather than at the same time).

2. *Accuracy Opposite-hand* — The same rules apply as given above except that each person throws with his/her left hand if he/she is right-handed and vice versa.

3. *Distance* — Each person throws against those in the same grade and of the same sex. Stretch your hose (or rope) out making a straight line. From behind the line all throw at the same time unless the group is small. A judge will determine whose frisbee went the greatest distance when it came to rest (the roll is included).

4. *Distance Opposite-handed* — The same rules apply as given above, except that each person throws with his left hand if he is right-handed and vice-versa.

5. *Boomerang* — All can compete together in this event. Have all the competitors line up in a straight line behind the marker

facing into the wind. At the signal everyone throws his frisbee at least fifteen feet into the air at an angle so that it will come back in a boomerang fashion. The person who throws the frisbee that returns closest to the throwing line is the winner.

6. *Frisbee Golf* — See *Ideas*, Volume 12

DOUBLES COMPETITION

1. *Single Frisbee Catch* — Have the participants pick a partner with whom they can compete. Two markers are stretched parallel to each other about fifteen feet apart. One partner stands behind one marker and the other partner stands behind the other marker directly opposite him. Only one frisbee is needed for each pair. Have all the frisbees on one side. At the signal all of those on one side throw their frisbees to their partners on the other side, who must catch it without crossing the marker. Those who do not catch it leave the game with their partner. After each throw one marker is moved back about three feet.

2. *Opposite-handed Single Frisbee Catch* — The same rules apply as given above, except that each person throws with his left hand if he is right-handed and vice versa.

3. *Double Frisbee Catch* — This is somewhat more difficult than the above events. Keeping the same partners, have each person take a frisbee. Again make two parallel lines but about ten feet apart. The rules are the same as the "single frisbee catch" except that each person throws his frisbee at the same time and each partner must catch the other's frisbee. Emphasize that *all* frisbees are to be thrown at the same time when the signal is given.

4. *Opposite-handed Double Frisbee Catch* — This is *very* challenging, but by now the participants have had practice. The same rules apply as given above, except that each person throws with his opposite hand.

5. *Doubles' Distance* — One partner from each pair lines up at a starting point. Each throws the frisbee as far as possible in a straight line away from the starting point. Then his partner stands exactly where the frisbee landed, and at the signal each of the other partners throws the frisbee as far as possible. The pair with the greatest combined distance is the winner.

TEAM COMPETITION

1. *Frisbee Relay* — Divide the group into teams of five to ten each. The team members form a straight line with approximately ten to fifteen yards between each member. The object is for the first person on each team to throw the frisbee to the second person

and on down the line — then back to the beginning. However, the team members *cannot* move to catch it. One foot must be stationary at all times. If the frisbee cannot be caught without moving both feet, then the team member who threw it must retrieve it and throw it again from his original position. (A frisbee or two may be started from each end to make the event more difficult.)

2. *Opposite-handed Frisbee Relay* — The same rules apply as given above, except that each person throws with his opposite hand.

(Contributed by Samuel Hoyt, Lansing, Michigan)

FUGITIVE

This is a simple, but good camp game played at night, and is much like "hide and seek." The group is divided into two teams: the Fugitives and the FBI. The FBI agents are equipped with flashlights. The Fugitives are given several minutes to hide. After the time limit is up, the FBI agents try to find the Fugitives. The Fugitives have a certain amount of time (anywhere from 10 to 30 minutes) in which they must reach "home base" (or "Mexico," etc.) which can be any designated area. If a Fugitive has a light shined on him and has his name called out as he attempts to hide or reach home base, then he goes to jail. If he makes it to home base, the Fugitive (team) gets 10 points. If he is caught by the FBI, then the FBI gets the 10 points. If the "home base" is a cabin, or a flagpole, etc., then it would be wise to set a distance of 25 to 40 feet around home base which is "off limits" to FBI agents. To make the game more difficult, arm the FBI agents with water balloons or squirt guns which they must hit Fugitives with before making an arrest. If the kids don't know each other's names, then the FBI agents can simply call out some other identifying trait, clothing, or whatever. After one game, play again with the teams reversing roles. (Contributed by Fred Winslow, Allen, Texas)

FUNNY BUNNY

This is a great travel game that can be used to make those long miles on youth trips go by at a rapid pace. Everyone can participate at the same time, either by giving clues for the game or trying to guess the answer. The game goes like this — Someone begins by giving a *two word clue,* such as "distant light" and then it is up to the rest of the participants to guess the answer. The *answer must be two rhyming words.* In the case of this illustration the answer to "distant light" would be "far star". The game continues with everyone participating until you arrive at your destination, run out of two word phrases, or just simply go out of your mind. There are literally hundreds of combinations, but here are just a few to get you started.

Clue	Answer
1. Distant Light	Far Star
2. Chef's Delight	O.K. Soufflé
3. Royal Hawk	Regal Eagle
4. White Spike	Pale Nail
5. Pig Chaser	Hog dog
6. Bench Fur	Chair Hair
7. Log Cover	Wood Hood
8. Distant Auto	Far Car
9. Enjoyable Jog	Fun Run
10. Tiny Insect	Wee Flea
11. Bed Plunder	Bunk Junk
12. Street Frog	Road Toad
13. Sack Label	Bag Tag
14. Important Path	Main Lane
15. Lemon Desert	Yellow Jello
16. Thin Coin	Skinny Penny
17. Tidy Chair	Neat Seat
18. Branch Notch	Stick Nick
19. False Pond	Fake Lake
20. Mop Closet	Broom Room
21. Ski-Slope Rake	Snow Hoe
22. Pale Watercolors	Faint Paint
23. Old Antler	Worn Horn
24. Chubby Insect	Fat Gnat
25. Sliced Acorn	Cut Nut
26. Dark Plunge	Dim Swim
27. Thin Spear	Narrow Arrow
28. Wet Postage	Damp Stamp
29. Cap Tap	Hat Pat
30. Ordinary Locomotive	Plain Train
31. Correct Evening	Right Night
32. Letter Bucket	Mail Pail
33. Pokey Pull	Slow Tow
34. Lengthy Melody	Long Song
35. Ranch Siren	Farm Alarm
36. Tire Noise	Wheel Squeal
37. Poster Sentence	Sign Line
38. Plain Board	Blank Plank
39. Path Wind	Trail Gale
40. Mountain Fall	Hill Spill
41. Cookie Bag	Snack Sack
42. Attractive outfit	Cute Suit
43. Dish-Cloth Shovel	Towel Trowel
44. Lettuce Song	Salad Ballad
45. Blender Repairer	Mixer Fixer
46. Specific Drapes	Certain Curtain

(Contributed by Terry McIlvain and Martha Sager, Wichita, Kansas)

HAPPY HANDFUL RELAY

This relay can be easily adapted for indoor or outdoor use. Assemble two identical sets of at least 12 miscellaneous items (i.e., 2 brooms, 2 balls, 2 skillets, 2 rolls of bathroom tissue, 2 ladders, etc.). Use your imagination to collect an interesting variety of identical pairs of objects. Place the two sets of objects on two separate tables.

Line up a team for each table. The first player for each team runs to his table, picks up one item of his choice, runs back to his team and passes the item to the second player. The second player carries the first item back to the table, picks up another item and carries both items back to the third player. Each succeeding player carries the items collected by his teammates to the table, picks up one new item and carries them all back to the next player. The game will begin rapidly, but the pace will slow as each player decides which item to add to a growing armload of items. It will also take increasingly longer for one player to pass his burden to the next player in line.

Once picked up, an item cannot touch the table or floor. Any item which is dropped in transit or transfer must be returned to the table by the leader. No one may assist the giving and receiving players in the exchange of items except through coaching. The first team to empty its table wins. (Contributed by Ed Stewart, Glendale, California)

HEADS UP

Here's a fun game that can be done as a team relay or simply for individual competition. You will need to make top hats for each participant or team, and you will need some string, ribbon (to tie the hats onto the players' heads), and plastic blocks or small lightweight balls.

Tie a block or ball to the end of each piece of string (about 30 inches long). Then tie the other end to the brim of each hat. The top should be open on each hat so that it can be used to catch the block. Use the ribbon to tie the hats on the players' heads so that the hats won't fall off. Now, each person stands with their hands behind their backs and tries to swing the block or ball into the top of

the hat. They may do anything to get it in except use their hands. Hats can be made out of poster board and cardboard. (Contributed by Dave Gilliam, Grove, Oklahoma)

HOOK-UP

An active game, Hook-up works best with ten or more people. Divide into pairs, have the partners link elbows and form a circle of pairs with at least four feet separating each pair from another. Then choose one person to be the "chaser" and another to be the "chasee". The chaser attempts to tag the chasee while running inside, outside and weaving through the circle of pairs. The chasee, anytime he wants to, can "pull into the pits" by grabbing the free elbow of one of the pairs. Doing so makes the chasee safe and takes him out of the chase and makes the person on the other side of the one whose elbow he grabbed the chasee. If the chasee is tagged, he becomes the chaser and the chaser becomes the chasee. (Contributed by Marshall Shelley, Elgin, Illinois)

HORSEY BACK TAG

This is a wild game that should be played on a grassy area. Each team is made up of a horse and rider. The rider "mounts" the horse by jumping on the back of the horse with arms around the horse's neck. Each rider has a piece of masking tape placed on their back by the leader so that it is easily seen and reached. When the signal "mount up" is given, the riders mount their horses and attempt to round up the tape on the other riders' backs. The last rider left with tape on his back wins. Only the riders may take the tape off other riders, the horses are just horses and if a horse falls, then that horse and rider are out of the game. (Contributed by Carl Campbell, Hunting- ton Valley, Pennsylvania)

HULA HOOPLA

The "hula-hoop" will never die. It has been around for quite a few years and should be around quite a few more. In light of this incredible truth, here are a few "hula-hoop relays" that can be a lot of fun. Divide into teams and run these relays in normal relay fashion. Each team should have a hula-hoop.

1. Place a hula-hoop on the floor 20 feet or so in front of each team. The object is for each player to run to the hoop, pick it up, and "hula" it around five or ten times (you decide how many), drop it to the floor and return to the line.

2. The object of this relay is for each person to take a hula-hoop and "hula" it while walking or running to a certain point 20 feet or so from the team and back. If the hula-hoop drops, the player must stop, get the hoop going again, and continue.

3. Place the hoop 20 feet or so away from the team once again. This time the player must run to the hoop and try to pass it over his body without using his hands. In other words, he must stand in the hoop and work it up and over his head with just his feet, legs, arms, etc., but no hands.

4. This relay is similar to the one above only two or three people run to the hoop at the same time, and without hands work the hoop up around their waists. They then run to a point and back with the hoop in place around their waists. At no time may their hands be used to hold the hoop up.

(Contributed by Cary F. Smith, Rusk, Texas)

INNER TUBE ROLL RELAY

This challenging game can be played indoors or out-of-doors. Divide the group into teams with an even number of people on each team. Then each team has its members pair up. The first couple from each team stands behind the starting line. A large inflated inner tube (preferably a bus or truck tire inner tube) is placed on the floor between them. At the sound of the whistle the couple must stand the tube up and together roll it around a chair and back to the starting line without using their hands. If the inner tube falls while they are rolling it they must come back to the starting line and begin again. They are not allowed to kick the inner tube along in a lying down position. When the couple successfully completes their round trip, the next couple places the tube flat on the floor and without using their hands they stand it up and "keep on tubin'." The first team to have all of its couples successfully complete the relay is the winner. If a team does not have an even number someone can go twice. The couples do not need to be of the opposite sex.
(Contributed by Samuel Hoyt, Lansing, Michigan)

JUMPING CATAPULT

This game could be set up permanently outside and could become a year-round challenge whenever things get boring. Set up a catapult (see diagram) with a ring drawn on the ground a few feet away. Using a playground ball, the kids then try to catapult the ball to the center of the ring. The closest one wins. (Contributed by Paul Warder, Monroe, Wisconsin)

KNIFE, FORK AND SPOON GAME

This is a simple "mindreading" game and yet one which can take up a good deal of time depending upon the alertness of the participants. To play, you will need a knife, a fork, a spoon, and a youth group. Have kids sit in a circle on the floor. Explain the game (secretly) to another person and begin.

Send your partner out of the room and tell the kids that they should pick someone sitting in the circle. Then tell them that you will communicate with your partner by what you do so that he will know who was chosen to be "it." Place the knife, fork, and spoon in any arrangement you choose in the middle of the circle on the floor, and then pick a place in the circle to sit. The key to communicating who is "it" to your partner has nothing to do with the knife, fork, and spoon, but in the fact that you assume a sitting position which is exactly like that of "it." If "it" moves to a different position to be more comfortable, so do you. Your partner makes a big deal about the knife, fork, and spoon, but picks up his clues from what you do, which is what you told the kids in your initial instructions. The knife, fork, and spoon are merely diversionary in that the kids assume what you do is limited to the knife, fork, and spoon. After your partner picks "it" to the total amazement of the group, the process is repeated until someone catches on. If someone feels they know the answer, they then go out of the room and become your partner. Depending upon the alertness of the group, this can continue until most everyone has had a chance to figure out the key to the game. (Contributed by Woody Weilage, Wichita Falls, Texas)

MAGAZINE SCAVENGER HUNT

Divide your group into teams of two or three persons each and give each group a combination of old magazines. Then give them a list of various items, photos, names, etc., that could be found in the magazines. As soon as a group finds one of the items, they cut it out and collect as many as they can in the time limit. The list can be long or short depending on the time. Some of the items will be found in several magazines while others in only one. You can make the list as difficult as you want. The winner, of course, is the team with the most items found. (Contributed by Michael Thiel, Everett, Washington)

MATCH UP

This is a variation of the old television game show "The Match Game." Divide into two or more teams of equal number. Have each team choose a team captain who goes to the front of the room with the other team captain(s). Everyone, including the team captains, should have several sheets of paper and pencils.

The leader then asks the entire group a question, such as "Who is going to win the World Series this year?" Everyone, without any discussion, writes his or her answer down on one slip of paper, and passes it in to the team captain, who has also written down an answer. When ready, the team captains announce their answers, and a point is awarded to each team for every answer from that team which matches their team captain's. In other words, if the team captain answered, "The Dodgers," then his or her team would get a point for every other answer from that team which also was "The Dodgers."

Some sample questions: *(Make up your own.)*

1. If you were going to repaint this room, what color would you do it in?
2. What country in the world would you most like to visit?
3. Your favorite T.V. show?
4. A number between one and five?
5. What book of the Bible has the most to say about good works?
6. What's the best way to have fun in this town?
7. What's the funniest word you can think of?
8. How many kids do you think you will have in your life?

(Contributed by Rick McPeak, Gresham, Oregon)

MATTRESS STUFF

Here's a good game for camps. It requires the use of those thin, lumpy mattresses that are common at most camps. You will also need a hole which you can cut in a sheet of plywood the size of a basketball hoop. Or you can use a basketball hoop.

The hole should be about hip high. Two people have to stuff the mattress through the hole without the use of their hands or arms. It takes team work and some hilarious wiggles. If used with teams, use several mattresses (and holes) at once and compete relay-style. (Contributed by Dave Gilliam, Grove, Oklahoma)

MONKEY SOCCER

For a fast-action outdoor game, designate a rectangular area of grass as a "monkey soccer" field, with a width of at least three feet per youth. Divide the youth into two teams, and provide one ball, volleyball size, but quite a light weight.

Here are the rules:

1. The object of each play is for the team which has the ball to get it across the other team's end of the court.

2. However, the ball must be kept either on the ground or else no higher off the ground than the height of the average player's knees.

3. Moreover, players may propel the ball only by reaching down and hitting it with their hands (clenched fists or otherwise). While in motion, the ball may bounce off a player, even off his or her foot while the player is running, but the player may not intentionally kick the ball or strike it with any part of the body except the hands.

4. Whenever the ball is kicked, or travels higher than a player's knees, or is held, it is placed on the grass where the foul occurred and put into play by the team opposing the team whose player committed the foul.

5. Whenever the ball leaves the court on a side, it is put into play at the point where it left the court by the team opposing the team whose player last touched the ball while it was still in play.

6. Teams may organize themselves in any way they desire to best protect their end of the court. Each team earns one point when its players get the ball over the opposing team's end of the court. The winning team is the first one to gain seven points.

(Contributed by John Bristow, Seattle, Washington)

MUDDY MARBLE SCRAMBLE

Here's a wild game for hot weather and large groups. Churn up a mud hole (figure approximately I to 2 square feet per kid). Then work hundreds of different colored marbles into the top 5 or 6 inches of mud. (Make sure the mud is without too many rocks.) Each different colored marble is worth a different amount of points. The fewer you have of one color, the more points they are worth. For example:

> 1 red marble: 500 points
> 2 white marbles: 100 points each
> 25 blue marbles: 50 points each
> 100 green marbles: 20 points each

Divide the group up into teams, each with two leaders - one who washes off the recovered marbles, the other keeps track of how many of each color have been recovered. At the signal, all of the participants dive in the mud and search for marbles for 10-15 minutes. When time is called, the team with the most points wins. (Contributed by Ted Thisse, Leesburg, Florida)

MUSICAL SQUIRT GUN

This exciting game can be played with a group ranging from six to thirty, indoors or out-of-doors. Have the group sit in a circle either on chairs or on the floor. A "loaded" squirt gun is passed around the circle until the music stops or until the leader says "Stop." The person who is holding the squirt gun at that time must leave the game. But before he leaves, he may squirt the person on his left twice or on his right twice or one each. After his chair is removed, the circle moves in a bit and the game continues. The last person left is declared the winner. (This game is a modification of "Musical Pies," Volume 13, *Ideas*, but a lot less messy).

Note: The gun must be passed with two hands and received with two hands or else it will be frequently dropped and will break. Also, it works best to have a second "loaded" squirt gun on hand to be substituted for the one which becomes empty. An assistant can then refill the original gun while the second one is being used. Be sure to emphasize that only two squirts are allowed. Otherwise you will be continually refilling the squirt guns. This is an exciting game. As teens are eliminated they will be "gunnin'" for a particular person and you will not be able to "water down" the excitement. (Contributed by Samuel Hoyt, Lansing, Michigan)

MUSICAL WASHTUBS

Here's a refreshing game for those hot days. First of all, you will need to secure the use of several large wash tubs, no small trick if you live in the suburbs. Then you fill the tubs with water and arrange them in a circle. Now the game is just like musical chairs. You have one more person than you have wash tubs, and while the "music" plays, everyone marches around the tubs. When the music stops (or a whistle is blown, etc.), each person must find a tub and sit in it - all the way. The person without a tub is eliminated. One tub is removed and the game continues until only one tub remains and two people must fight for it. The winner is whoever winds up in the last tub. As the game progresses, it will be necessary to have some- one with a hose (or two) to keep the tubs full of water. A variation would be to fill the tubs with mud. (Contributed by Bob Messer, Hurst, Texas)

NERF BASEBALL

This is a great inside winter night activity. All that is needed is a "Nerf" Baseball (3 ½ inches in diameter), a "Whipple" Bat, and a room large enough for the bases. (Nerf Baseballs and Whipple Bats can be found in most toy stores.) The bases are placed 25 feet apart and they are 1 ½ foot masking tape squares. The pitcher's mound is about 15 feet from home plate. All the rules are the same as regular baseball except that the runner can be put out if he isn't on the base and is hit by the Nerf Ball. (Contributed by Michael Thiel, Everett, Washington)

NERF FOOTBALL LEAGUE

Now your youth group can have its very own "N.F.L." This crazy version of football can be played indoors with almost any number of kids. You could divide into teams and have a "Nerf Football Tourna- ment," with the Super Bowl as its climax. Here's the way the game is played.

1. Basic football rules are in force. The object is to score touch- downs. Your football field should be marked with boundaries, goal lines, etc.

2. There is absolutely no running or fast walking allowed. The "officials" can determine penalties for this. All players must walk when the ball is in play.
3. There are only four downs allowed. No first downs. If you can't score a TD in four, then the ball is turned over to the other team.
4. Passing can be in any direction to any player on your team. There can be more than one pass per down. In other words, players can keep passing the ball until someone is finally tagged by an opposing player.
5. No tackling. This should be two-hand touch anywhere, or "flag" football.
6. Don't replay "interference" calls. Low ceilings, furniture, etc., are all part of the game. Adapt the rules to whatever environment you have.
7. The ball must be a soft, spongy "Nerf" ball (available in any toy store) or something similar.

(Contributed by Jeff Dietrich, Amesbury, Massachusetts)

NERFKETBALL

Here is a fun version of basketball using a "nerf" ball (soft sponge) and chairs. Choose two teams of equal numbers and seat them alternately on sturdy chairs as shown in the diagram: two rows of players facing each other. For best results, players should be spaced at least double arm's distance apart both sideways and across. Place a "basket" (small bucket, gallon plastic bottle with top cut off, etc.) at each end of the double row, approximately six feet from the players at the ends of the rows. The basket should also be on the floor.

The two basic ground rules of the game are : (1) Chairs cannot be moved or tipped; (2) Each player must remain seated while the ball is in play.

Using a coin flip, one team is chosen to take first possession of the ball. Play begins as the player farthest from his team's goal is given the ball by the referee. The team tries to work the ball toward their goal by passing it while opponents try to block passes and steal the ball. Any player may take a shot at the goal at any time, but the advantages of passing the ball to the player nearest the goal are obvious. If the ball is intercepted by the other team, play continues in the opposite direction.

When an attempted field goal misses, the ball is automatically "out" to the other team and play then goes the other way. When a field goal is scored, all players rotate one seat to the right. This will give each player the opportunity to be his team's prime shooter during the game. After rotation, the ball goes "out" to the other team and goes the other way.

Any ball loose within the playing area is a free ball. Any ball going outside the playing area is given to the player nearest the last player to touch the ball.

Penalties may be assessed and free throws awarded for players leaving their seats or unnecessary roughness. Limit the game by using a kitchen timer for quarters or halves, or by setting a scoring limit. (Contributed by Ed Stewart, Glendale, California)

NEW VOLLEYBALL

Here is a great new way to play the old game of volleyball. "New Volleyball" can be played on a regular volleyball court, with the normal amount of players on each team. A regular volleyball is used as well. The main difference is the scoring.

The object of the game is for a team to volley the ball as many times as possible without missing or fouling (up to 50 times) before hitting it back over the net to the opposing team who will make every attempt to return it without missing. If they do miss, the opposite team receives as many points as they volleyed before sending it over the net. All volleys must be counted audibly by the entire team (or by scorers on the sidelines) which aids in the scoring process and also helps build tension. So the idea is to volley the ball as many times as possible each time the ball comes over the net, and then to safely return it back over the net and hope that the other team blows it.

Other rules for this game as follows:

1. No person may hit the ball two consecutive times.
2. No two people may hit the ball back and forth to each other more than once in succession to increase the number of volleys. In other words, player A may hit it to player B, but Player B may not hit it back to player A. Player A may hit it again once someone else has hit it besides player B.
3. Five points are awarded to the serving team if the opposing team fails to return a serve.
4. Five points are awarded to the receiving team if a serve is missed (out-of-bounds, in the net, etc.)
5. Players rotate on each serve, even if the serving team scores on successive serves.

6. A game is fifteen minutes. The highest score wins.
7. All other volleyball rules are in effect.

(Contributed by Norma Bailey, Colora, Maryland)

NO TRESPASSING

Tie a plastic-covered clothesline rope, approximately 20 feet long, to two folding chairs, so that the rope is about 8 inches off the floor. The rope should be in the center of the room. Also, be sure and mark your rope with a masking tape flag approximately one foot from each chair. This is for the safety of whoever is "it."

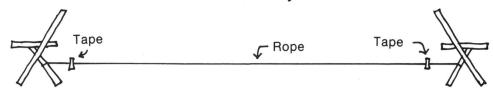

Choose one person to be "it" and divide the rest into two groups. Each group takes one end of the field (or room) facing the other group. Blindfold the "it" person and also give him some knee pads to protect his knees if the floor is hard or rough. The "it" person then takes his position, kneeling with one hand on the rope. He is free to move on his knees as long as he is touching the rope. On a signal each team hops on one foot across the rope to get to the other side. Team members must cross the rope without tripping or being tagged by the person who is "it." Before jumping over the rope, each person must announce his jump by clapping his hands together five times. Any "trespassers" (jumpers) caught become an obstacle for the next round. They lie face down parallel to the rope, leaving room on each side for the jumpers. The first person caught becomes the next "it." (Contributed by Tom Bougher, Grand Junction, Colorado)

ONE FOOT STAND

Here's a game that sounds very simple, but isn't. All each individual has to do is stand on one foot while holding the other with his eyes closed. The one who can do it the longest is the winner. It is doubtful anyone will be able to do this for as much as thirty seconds. (Contributed by Ron Erber, Hannover, North Dakota)

PAPER SHOOT

Divide into teams of from four to eight kids each. Set a garbage can up in the middle of the room (about three feet high), and prepare ahead of time several paper batons and a lot of wadded up paper balls. One team lies down around the trash can with their heads toward the can (on their backs). Each of these players has a paper baton. The opposing team stands around the trash can behind a line about ten feet or so away from the can. This line can be a large circle drawn around the can. The opposing team tries to throw wadded up paper balls into the can, and the defending team tries to knock the balls away with their paper batons while lying on their backs. The opposing team gets two minutes to try and shoot as much paper into the can as possible. After each team has had its chance to be in both positions, the team that got the most paper balls into the can is declared the winner. To make the game a bit more difficult for the throwers, have them sit in chairs while they toss the paper. (Contributed by Jeff Dietrich, Amesbury, Massachusetts)

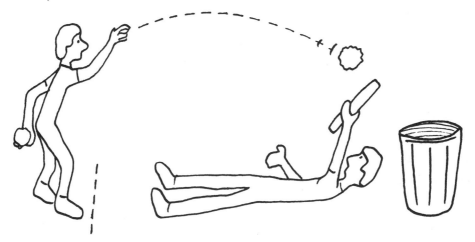

PEANUT BUTTER RELAY

Teams line up single file. Each team should have an equal number of players. A glob of peanut butter (or other such gooey substance) is placed on the person's nose at the end of each line. He then passes the glob to the next person and so on down the line. Prizes are awarded for speed and for the biggest glob on the last person's nose. Only for groups with strong stomachs or long tongues. (Contributed by Dave Phillips, Old Greenwich, Connecticut)

PEANUT BROOM SWEEP RELAY

Have two teams line up in a shuttle formation (one half of the team lines up single file behind a line; the other half lines up behind a second line facing them). The first person in one line of each team is given a broom (children's broom or regular). A small pile of peanuts is piled in front of him. On the whistle, the person with the broom sweeps peanuts to the opposite line, gives the broom to the first person in that line. This person in turn sweeps the peanuts back to the other line until all the contestants in both lines have taken their turns. The first team finished wins. (Contributed by Norma Bailey, Colora, Maryland)

PINCH ME

Here's a wild game that is great for dividing a large group into smaller groups. Everyone is to remain silent (no talking, but laughing, screaming, etc. is permitted). Each person receives a slip of paper which he is to keep secret from everyone else. The papers all read something like:

Pinch Me
Slap Me
Tickle Me
Step on My Toes
Rub My Tummy
Scratch My Back
Pull My Ear

When everyone has a card, the leader yells "go" and the players must find the others in their group. For instance, a "Pinch Me" must go around pinching everyone until he finds someone else who is a "Pinch Me." They stick together pinching others until they find the rest of their team. There should be an equal number of each group. After a period of time, the leader stops the game, and the team that has done the best job of getting together wins. (Contributed by David Garda, Elmhurst, Illinois)

PING PONG BALL FLOAT

For this relay, you will need coffee cans (empty), ping pong balls, buckets of water, towels, and one guy with his shirt off for every team participating.

The guy with his shirt off lies on his back about ten yards from his team who are in a single-file line. Place the coffee can (empty) on his stomach or chest. Put the ping pong ball in the coffee can. A bucket full of water goes beside each team.

As the game begins, players use their cupped hands to carry water from their bucket to the coffee can. Each player goes one at a time. As the coffee can fills with water, the ping pong ball rises in the can. As soon as it is high enough, a player tries to remove it from the can with his mouth. The first team to get the ping pong ball out of the can (no hands) and back across the finish line, wins. (Contributed by Larry Jansen, Indianapolis, Indiana)

PYRAMID CLUMPS

This game is very similar to CLUMPS (Ideas Number One) with a fun little twist. Have your kids mill around the floor. Then the leader blows the whistle or horn and yells out any number. After the number is called, the participants seek out the called number of kids, get down on their hands and knees and build a "pyramid." The pyramid group must have exactly the called number of kids or they are out of the game. Extra people are also out. The game continues until one individual or one small group remains. (Contributed by Norma Bailey, Colora, Maryland)

RING AROUND THE RIND

This is a great idea for a picnic or day at the park activity. Slice a watermelon like a loaf of bread and pass out the circular sections to each member of the group. Explain that each person must eat their piece without their hands touching any thing but the rind and without breaking the slice. When finished, only a green ring of rind should remain. The object is to be the first person to finish eating the inside of the circle. You can offer a prize for the winner - a towel for their dripping chin. (Contributed by Marshall Shelley, Elgin, Illinois)

RUB MY BACK AND I'LL RUB YOURS

Everyone pairs off. Clip a number of clothespins on each person's back (the same number for each player). They should be clipped to their shirt or coat tails, or wherever there is some loose clothing. On "go," the partners rub backs, and try to knock all the clothespins off without using hands. The first to do so is the winner. (Contributed by Dave Gilliam, Grove, Oklahoma)

SARDINES

This game is quite similar to "hide and seek." The group chooses one person to be "it." This person hides while the rest of the group counts to 100 (or a signal is given). Now the group sets out to find the hidden person. Each person should look individually, but small groups, say of two or three, may look together. When a person finds "it," he or she hides with "it" instead of telling the rest of the group. The hiding place may be changed an unlimited number of times during any game. The last person to find the hidden group, which has now come to resemble a group of "sardines," is the loser or "it" for the next game. (Contributed by G. Neale Wirtanen, Arlington, Virginia)

SHOE HOCKEY

Here's an active group game that should be played inside on a large smooth floor. It's a new version of hockey, played with one shoe off and one shoe on. The "one shoe off" becomes the player's "hockey stick." The kids should be instructed to wear soft soled shoes. A sock stuffed with cloth and tied closed becomes the "puck." Each team should have five players at a time on the playing field. The floor should be marked to indicate boundaries, a mid-court line, and the goals on each end. Lines can be marked with masking tape.

The rules are as follows:

1. Each player uses one of his or her shoes as a hockey stick while wearing the other shoe and both socks.
2. The puck may be stopped by any part of a person's body, but it may be propelled only by a player's hockey stick (shoe).
3. The court is divided in the middle, with three members of each team restricted to their end of the room to guard the goal, while the other two members of each team are restricted to the opposing team's end of the room.
4. The game is started by lining up the five players on one side (three of that side's team with two of the other team) facing the five on the other side, at least ten feet away from the center spot. The referree places the puck on the center mark, backs away a safe distance, and calls the game into play.
5. Whenever the puck goes into the goal, even if it was hit by the wrong team, it scores a point for the offensive team.
6. Fouls are called whenever a player hits another player with his shoe, knocks another player's shoe out of his hand, leaves his restricted area, or when a player propells the puck with anything other than the "hockey stick." Players may be suspended from the game (placed in the penalty box) or the opposing team can simply take a "free shot" at the goal from mid-court.

(Contributed by John Bristow, Seattle, Washington)

SLAP SLAP

In this game, if directions are followed correctly, height, weight, or sex need not be a factor to win. Simply have two players face each other and raise their hands above their shoulders and then match hands. A distance of 18 to 36 inches may separate the players, but as the players match hands, they should be able to push each other's hands and arms back and forth comfortably (always above the shoulders). At the signal, the players attempt to slap or push the other's hands so as to force the other off balance. The first person to loose their balance or move either foot, gives way to another challenger with the winner staying in. (Contributed by Ron Erber, Hannover, North Dakota)

SMUGGLER

This is a great camp game that is relatively complicated and requires the use of the entire camp area (several acres or so.) There are two teams (any number on a team), two "territories" (divide the camp in half) and each team should be appropriately marked (colored armbands, etc.). The idea of the game is to smuggle certain items into the other team's territory successfully (without being captured) and make a "drop." Points are awarded for successful drops and for capturing smugglers.

The playing area should look something like this:

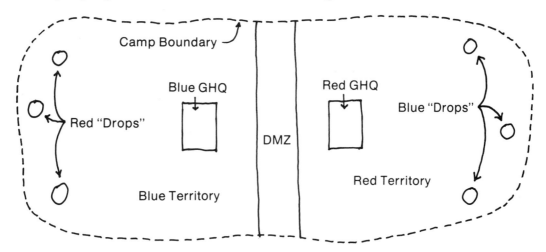

Teams should have names or be designated by color (i.e. Red Army, Blue Army). Each team selects up to 25% of its players (number can vary) to be "smugglers." They are so identified with an "S" marked on the back of their hands with a felt tipped pen. They are the only ones who are allowed to smuggle items into the other team's territory. The rest of the team may capture smugglers from the other team. Smugglers may not capture anyone. Each team should also have a "general" who is "in charge," coordinates team strategy, and remains at all times in the "GHQ" (General's headquarters).

Camp staff and counselors are neutral and are called "U.N. Observers." They are positioned on the two teams' territories to maintain order, offer advice, and make sure everyone is playing by the rules of the game. One U.N. Observer on each side should be assigned the task of keeping score for that side.

One interesting twist to this game is that each team is allowed a certain number of "infiltrators" or spies who wear the armbands of one team, but are actually working for the other team. They can be chosen by the game officials prior to the game and secretly informed of their mission. Infiltrators are secretly marked with an "X" (or anything) on one leg (or some other place that is relatively hidden). If a player is accused of being an infiltrator, he must show his leg, and tell the truth. If the accusation is correct, the accusing team gets 5,000 points and the infiltrator is taken into custody. He must remain in the GHQ for 10 minutes and is then released to the team he is working for. He gets a new armband and is back in the game, only not as an infiltrator. An incorrect accusation costs the accusing team 5,000 points (points lost). Note: Only the general of each team may make an accusation. If a player suspects a teammate to be a spy, the general is informed and he decides whether or not to accuse. Then the accusation must be made in the presence of a U.N. Observer.

The "drops" are locations (under rocks, in trees, etc.) where a smuggled item may be placed, upon which it may be declared successfully smuggled. Only the smuggling team knows where all the drops are in the opposing team's territory. In other words, the blue team does not know where the red team is attempting to drop items, and vice-versa. However, before the game begins, each team locates their drop positions in the other team's territory, and a game official (neutral person) informs the opposing team's general as to the location of half of them. So, the blue team, for example, might know where half of the red team's drops are, and the red team isn't sure which ones they know about. There should be at least four drops for each side (any number without getting ridiculous). U.N. Observers should know where all the drop locations are.

The "DMZ" is a neutral area that is marked off between the two territories. Anyone may be there without being captured. This is good for strategy, but may be optional.

The game should be played at night. No flashlights are allowed. Because the entire camp is used, buildings, trees, and other obstacles may be used for cover. Unsafe areas should be declared off-limits. Players caught in an off-limits area should be penalized by subtracting 5,000 points off their team's score.

The items to be smuggled are simply 3 X 5 cards with the name of the item on it and its value.

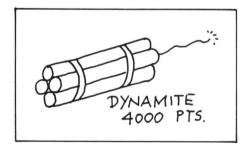

DYNAMITE
4000 PTS.

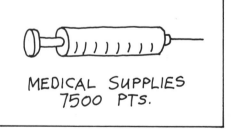

MEDICAL SUPPLIES
7500 PTS.

Different items are worth more than others. Points should range anywhere from 1,000 points to 10,000 points. There should be more items of lower point value with the high scoring items being more "rare." Any number of items may be used in the game, as long as each team has the same number with the same values. The red team's items should be written in red ink, and vice-versa.

As the game progresses, smugglers attempt to get items behind enemy lines and successfully "dropped" at one of the drop locations in enemy territory. Only one item may be smuggled at one time by a smuggler. Once a drop is made (successfully), the smuggler raises his hand and yells "U.N.'" until he finds or is found by a U.N. Observer. The U.N. Observer then verifies the drop and escorts him back to his own territory where points are awarded. While a smuggler has his hand raised and is yelling "U.N.," he may not be captured by the enemy. Faking this procedure is a rule infraction that costs you 5,000 points.

If the smuggler is captured during his smuggling attempt, he is brought to the GHQ of the capturing team and must remain there for 10 minutes before being released. (This time can vary.) He also gets a mark on his hand in the capturing team's color. The mark keeps the capturing team up-to-date on how many times he has been caught. Every time a smuggler is captured, the appropriate score is tallied, and the smuggled item is confiscated.

In the face of imminent capture, a smuggler may dump or get rid of the item he is attempting to smuggle and hope that it will not be discovered or that it might be picked up by a fellow smuggler. If the capturing team finds it, they may turn it in for its face value.

Smugglers may be captured any number of ways, depending on how rough or messy you want to get. They may be tagged, tackled, hit with a water balloon, or perhaps hit with a nylon stocking full of flour. Choose your own method.

Scoring:

1. A successful drop is worth 1,000 points plus the value of the item.
2. An extra 2,000 points is earned if the smuggler can make a successful drop and return to his own team's territory without being captured by the enemy or escorted back by a U.N. Observer.
3. On capturing a smuggler, the capturing team gets points in the following manner.

    a. First time caught - 500 points plus half the value of the item being smuggled.

    b. Second time caught - 1500 points plus full value of item.

    c. Third time caught - 3000 points plus full value of item.

4. Correctly identifying an infiltrator is worth 5000 points. Incorrectly accusing one costs 5000 points.
5. Any "item" found bearing the opposing team's color may be

turned in for the full value of the item.

(Contributed by Keith Geckeler, Escondido, California)

SOCKER BOPPERS

Centsable Products, 560 Hicks Road, Palatine, Illinois 60067, offers an inflatable toy called "Socker Boppers" that can be used for all kinds of games. They allow hand to hand combat without risk of injury, and are an alternative to "Bataca Bats" (see *Ideas Number Seven*) If they are not available at a store near you.

Centsable also produces the "Silly Sword," which is a sword with a plastic inflatable blade, and is good for the many games in *Ideas* that require the use of rolled up newspapers, etc. Another Cent-

sable product is the "Body Bumper" which is an inflatable vest which allows kids to bump into each other without getting hurt. The Body Bumper protects the body and the head from any impact, so kids can run into each other "bumper car" style without injury. Write Centsable for a catalog, or check with your local toy store.

SPACE BALL COUNTDOWN

Here is a fast, exciting, and rough game that requires teamwork...and kids love it. Form two equal teams with one team forming an evenly spaced rectangle or circle and the other team inside the circle as dispersed as possible. When the whistle sounds, the team outside tries to hit with the ball (two playground balls, not soccer balls) every member inside as quickly as possible. Head hits and bounce hits are illegal.

When everyone has been hit, the clock stops, the time recorded and the teams change places. The team with the shortest time in the outside circle wins. You can score the best two out of three rounds or combine total times. Be sure to have players remove glasses, aim shoulder level and below, and do not use hard soccer-type balls. (Contributed by Norma Bailey, Colora, Maryland)

SQUAT

This game can really be fun, and if everything is not done quite right, it can be a spectacular flop. First of all, get everyone in a circle shoulder to shoulder. Then have everyone turn right, facing the back of the person in front of them. On the count of three, sit down.

If everything is done right, everyone will simultaneously sit down on the lap of the person behind him. If the timing isn't quite right...well. To make the game even more precarious, have everyone cross their right leg over their left before sitting down. Make sure everyone's hands are out to the side. (Contributed by Marshall Shelley, Elgin, Illinois)

STATIC SNOW

For an hysterical fun activity, have your youth group get together in a small room. In advance, buy several large bags of white styrofoam beads and funnel them into a vacuum cleaner. Then hook the hose on so the vacuum cleaner blows. (Be sure to run a test blow before adding the styrofoam beads or you will blow dust over everyone.) Turn on the machine and spray the beads all over the room. The feather weight beads become charged with static electricity and stick to everything and everyone. They are difficult to clean up, but the effect is worth it. For a little more excitement, you might turn all the lights out so that the kids have no idea what is being sprayed on them. (Contributed by Chip Sutton, Danvers, Massachusetts)

STICK IT

Here's a game of skill that can be played by as few as two people. You need the following items: two light ropes about 10 feet long, several dowels (round sticks) about 12 inches long, a box big enough for the dowels to go in, a chair and a lectern (speaker stand) or something similar.

Tack the two cords to the lectern two inches apart and stretch the ropes (cords or string) back to the chair, ten feet away. One person stands on the chair and holds the ropes. The box is placed approximately two-thirds of the way from the chair under the ropes. A second player places the dowels (one at a time) on the two ropes at the holder's hands, and the holder tries to roll the dowel down the ropes and then dump it into the box. If he fails, he must try again. Players can be timed (best time to get them all in) or two can be going at once for a good race. For team relays, each person gets a dowel, and they must all get their dowels in the box. Note: after you are through using the dowels, give them to the children's department to be used as rhythm sticks or for rolling out clay. (Contributed by Dave Gilliam, Grove, Oklahoma)

TABLE VOLLEYBALL

Divide into two teams (of course). Use either a regular volleyball or any other soft facsimile. This is for when you have to be indoors and you don't have room to play a real game of volleyball. Set tables on top of one another across the room. All participants must stay on their knees at all times. The ball is permitted to hit the ceiling. Otherwise, all normal rules of volleyball stand. Depending on the number of players on each team, you might permit one free bounce of the ball on each side before the ball must be returned over the net. The net, of course, is the stack of tables. (Contributed by Jim Walton, Wheaton, Illinois)

THROUGH THE LEGS SHUFFLE

Here's the old "through-the-legs" game with a new twist. Have the teams line up single file spreading their legs apart enough so that someone can crawl through them. Everyone must have their hands on the hips of the person in front of them. The lines must be behind the starting line. On the signal, the last person crawls through the legs of the team and stands up at the front of the line. As soon as they stand up, the person who is now at the rear of the line crawls through, etc. The line moves forward and the first team to cross the goal line wins. Only one person per team can be crawling at a time. (Contributed by Ken McCoy, Salem, Oregon)

TIRE GRAN PRIX

Lay out a course around the church buildings or down roads that are closed to traffic, and give everyone an old tire. Then have a race rolling the tires around the course. For larger groups, make it a team relay, with kids stationed every 50 yards along the course. The tire is passed on at each "pit stop" to a fresh "driver." The first player (or team) to complete the course wins.

For added fun, allow players to kick, knock over, or in any way impede the progress of the opposing racers. Old tires may be borrowed from a cooperative tire dealer or service station. (Contributed by Gene Poppino, Jr., Portland, Oregon)

TRASH CAN BASKETBALL

This is an indoor version of basketball that can be played when the real thing is not available. Set up large trash cans at each end of the room (kids love to shoot things into trash cans). Use a soft, children's ball about eight inches in diameter, or anything else that will work. Rules are all the same as normal basketball except for a few:

1. There is no dribbling. All movement of the ball is by passing. This helps to make the game not only more practical, but a lot fairer in the coed situation.
2. No running with the ball. You can only pass it to a teammate.
3. If you touch a player with the ball, that's a foul. The fouled player gets a free shot.
4. There should be a ring drawn around the trash cans about six feet out from the cans, which is a no-man's land. No one is allowed in this circle. That prevents goal tending and dunking, making the game a bit more fair for everyone.

(Contributed by Jim Walton, Wheaton, Illinois)

WAGON RELAY

For this team relay, you will need to obtain the use of one or more wagons (the type that most kids have, but not too small). Each team pairs off and a pair at a time, one person sits in the wagon and uses the handle to steer while the other person pushes him or her around a slalom course. When one couple finishes, the next begins, and the first team to have everyone complete the course wins.

A variation of this is to have one person ride in the wagon, just sitting there doing nothing, while the other person holds on to the handle and uses it both to steer and to push the wagon backwards through the course. It's not easy. (Contributed by Sam Walker, Sheboygan, Wisconsin)

WATER BALLOON VOLLEYBALL

Water Balloon Volleyball is played very similarly to a regular game of conventional volleyball. Set up your volleyball net as usual, and divide the young people into equal sides. This type of volleyball is not restricted to the conventional 6-member, 9-member team, but any number of young people may play. Of course, the main difference in this game is that instead of using a regular volleyball, you use a water balloon for the ball. The service takes place from the back line and each team is allowed three tosses and three catches in order to get the water balloon over the net to the opposing team. The opposing team then has three tosses and three catches in order to get the ball back across the net. The balloon is continually tossed back and forth across the net until, finally, breakage occurs. When the balloon breaks, the side on which it breaks does not score, but rather, the opposite team gets the point, without regard to who did the serving. Spikes are allowed, but again, if the balloon breaks on the team who is doing the spiking, the other team is awarded the point. The team that then wins the point, regardless of which team it is, is the team that continues to serve until service is broken. The game is played to a regular volleyball score of 15, at which time sides of the net are changed and the game resumes. All other rules in regular volleyball are in effect for this game, such as out-of-bound lines, not being able to cross over the net with your hand, or falling into the net with your body.

Another variation of this game which proves to be even more fun, is to include 30 or 40 members of each team and insert into play 4 or 5 water balloons, so that there are several opportunities for returns, spikes, and services all at the same time. The rules for this game are the same as for the one-ball system. There is no official scoring for this game. The winning team is simply the driest team at the end of an allotted period of time. (Contributed by Terry McIlvain, Wichita, Kansas)

WEIRD BARROW RACE

This is a variation of the old wheelbarrow race where player A becomes the wheelbarrow by walking on his hands while player B uses player A's feet as handles, and simply runs along behind. In this game, you do basically the same thing, but the added difficulty is that the wheelbarrow (player A) must push a volleyball along the ground with his nose. This can be done as a relay, with team members pairing off and pushing the ball around a goal and back. (Contributed by Burney Heath, Cape Coral, Florida)

WHEELBARROW OBSTACLE COURSE

Here's a great activity for an all day game event. Using a real wheelbarrow, blindfold the driver and have the person sitting in the wheelbarrow give directions through an obstacle course. (Contributed by Paul Warder, Monroe, Wisconsin

Chapter Three

Creative Communication

AIRPORT

If you have a large airport in your area, this could turn out to be a very thought provoking activity. Have your group break up into groups of two. Each duet is to decide on one person in the airport to follow for 45 minutes and make notes of their observations. At the end of the 45 minutes have the groups gather at a designated area and discuss the various people they observed. Discussion should include what the people were doing, what were their emotions, what clues did the people give you about themselves? What did you learn about non-verbal communication? (Contributed by Pastor David, Silver Spring, Maryland)

AMPLIFIED CONVERSATIONS

The phone company can install (for a slight fee, of course) a temporary amplified phone system by which a roomful of people can both listen and talk to people across the country with whom you wish to have conversations. This allows people in distant places to participate in your meeting by being interviewed (live) over the telephone in this manner. Line up the interviews, then call in the phone company. (Contributed by Bertram H. Rutan, Aberdeen, Washington)

ARMAGEDDON BOMBER

If played seriously, this can be a great discussion starter. Armageddon Bomber is a simulation game that can be done with several groups in different rooms. Each group should include four people (pilot, bombardier, radio controller, and co-pilot). Give the following information to each group:

The year is 1984. You are the flight team of an advanced, ultramodern U.S. bomber and you are flying maneuvers over the Atlantic. You suddenly receive a highly classified message which is coded and comes from a computer. (The message below should be given to each flight team in coded form. Make up your own code and give each group the key.)

EMERGENCY ALERT: CODE RED
U.S. HAS RECEIVED NUCLEAR ATTACK BY USSR.
CASUALTIES AND DESTRUCTION NOT KNOWN AT
THIS TIME. U.S. UNABLE TO RETALIATE . . . TOTAL
DESTRUCTION IS IMMINANT. YOU ARE CARRYING
ADVANCED NUCLEAR WARHEAD. ONLY HOPE.
YOUR LOCATION PINPOINTED HALF WAY BETWEEN
U.S. AND USSR. YOUR FUEL AT 50 PER CENT.
MAINTAIN RADIO SILENCE AND PROCEED WITH
OPERATION RANGER RED. DELIVER WARHEAD.

Each group has twenty minutes to decode the message and make a decision among themselves. The decision to fulfill the mission must be unanimous. If you decide not to fulfill the mission, your options are as follows:

1. You will change course and attempt to land in Greenland and hope the contamination has not reached you.
2. You will attempt to crash the plane in the target area rather than stay alive.
3. You will surrender to the enemy.
4. You will commit suicide and not drop the bomb.
5. You will simply keep flying and hope that you can get a clear picture of the situation and make up your mind at the last possible minute.
6. You will fly back to the U.S. and assess the damage. And hope that you can refuel somewhere.

After the time is up have each group share their decision and the reasons for it. Here are some possible questions:

1. Do the teachings of Jesus apply to this situation? If so, which ones?
2. How much of your decision was influenced by your Christian convictions?

(Contributed by Ed Woodard, Norfolk, Virginia)

AWARENESS OF OTHERS

Have one person in the group go out of the room for a short time (pick someone who doesn't embarrass very easily). Ask the rest of the group to describe what the person was wearing. Be as specific as possible. Then bring the person back in and let everyone see what he or she was wearing. Begin your session on awareness this way. Most groups will remember very little in specific terms about the clothing worn by the chosen person. From this you can talk about the shallowness of our everyday contacts with people. This can lead into a discussion of our ability as Christians to perceive other's needs and show that perception is the first step in ministering to a need. This also points out that noticing things about others is something that must be worked at. This discussion could also lead into Christ's perception of needs, how He relied on God the Father for help in this area, and what this means to our ability of perception. (Contributed by Bonnie Erb, Virginia Beach, Virginia)

BODY LANGUAGE

Lay a large cardboard cut in the shape of the human body, minus the head, on the floor. Then have the kids, equipped with colored marking pens, choose a part of the body that they feel represents them. They then write on that part of the body their name, or a symbol, or a phrase that relates to their choice. After everyone is done, each person shares why they chose the part of the body they did and the meaning of the symbol or phrase that related to their choice. At the end of the meeting, you can tape the body to a door and add a cut-out head of Christ. This can be very effective during a discussion of the Church, the Body, and I. Cor. 12:12-21. (Contributed by Richard Young, Hanford, California)

BROTHER HOOD HOUR

Here is a fun skit that can be used quite effectively as a discussion starter centered around the topic "The Body of Christ". Set up the stage area like a typical television "talk-show", and have the actors learn the lines well enough that they don't need scripts. Follow up with a discussion or study of 1 Corinthians 12:12-31.

Announcer: And now, from Hollywood ... it's (music) the Brother Hood Hour, featuring the inimitable Brother Johnny Hood himself! ... Here's Johnny!

Brother Hood: Thank you, thank you. (Applause) Thank you, thank you. (Applause) THANK YOU!! Have we got a show lined up for you! We have guests from around the world to discuss tonight's topic: Who or What is the Body of Christ. So let's get started and bring on our

68

first guest. And here he is, from Ringworm, Georgia, Mr. Foot!

Mr. Foot: Well, hello Brother Hood!

Brother Hood: Mr. Foot, I can't tell you what a pleasure it is to have you on our program.

Mr. Foot: I'm glad to be here, Brother. I bring you greetings from the N.A.E.F.

Brother Hood: I'm sorry, but I'm not familiar with the N.A.E.F.

Mr. Foot: A man of your caliber? I find that hard to believe! Well anyway, the N.A.E.F. is the National Association of Evangelical Feet, of which I am a charter member.

Brother Hood: Oh, yes! As I recall, your group has recently come out with a new paraphrase of the Bible.

Mr. Foot: Paraphrase my foot! This is a superior translation of the Bible!

Brother Hood: And what is it called?

Mr. Foot: Dr. Scholl's Authorized Version. It is truly a remarkable work. This man has studied widely. He speaks 11 foreign languages including Greek and Hebrew.

Brother Hood: Is this in any way related to the Odor Eaters' Translation?

Mr. Foot: No, no! The N.A.E.F. looks with disdain upon the Odor Eaters' Translation. In fact, we just think it stinks!

Brother Hood: Well, getting down to our topic, how do you, as a Foot, feel about the rest of the Body of Christ?

Mr. Foot: Well, as a group of Feet, we feel that we have been trampled on by the rest of the Body of Christ.

Brother Hood: And what makes you feel that way?

Mr. Foot: Let me answer that by telling you a little story. The other day at my country club . . .

Brother Hood: You belong to a country club?

Mr. Foot: Oh yes, Club Foot. Anyway, I ran into a woman that is in my Sunday School class. Do you know what she said to me? "Mr. Foot, you are a big heel!" Can you imagine that? I whipped around in holy anger and said, "Woman, you ain't got no soul!" It's just terrible the way we're treated as Feet.

Brother Hood: I agree, that is bad! But, who, would you say, makes up the Body of Christ?

Mr. Foot: Primarily Feet.

Brother Hood: Would you go as far as to say that to be a member of the Body you must be a Foot?

Mr. Foot: Are you trying to buttonhole me?!!

Brother Hood: Oh, no, Mr. Foot! But, surely, you must have some thoughts on the matter?

Mr. Foot: Well, I do. I do believe you must be a Foot to be a member of the Body of Christ.

Brother Hood: Thank you, Mr. Foot. I'd like to chat with you a bit more but I must bring on our next guest. Won't you welcome with a big hand, from La Salada, Guatemala, Señor Hand! (Applause)

Señor Hand: Buenos noches, Hermano Hood.

Brother Hood: Welcome, Señor Hand. Could you tell our audience what your occupation is?

Señor Hand: I am professor of religion at the La Salada Universitas de los Manos.

Brother Hood: I understand that the La Salada University of the Hands is a private school that grips the more traditional fundamentalist position. Is that true?

Señor Hand: Sí.

Brother Hood: How do the Hands feel about the Body of Christ?

Señor Hand: I'm so glad that you asked that question, señor. We feel that, as Hands, we aren't getting a fair shake in the body of Christ. For some reason, we're always in hot water!

Brother Hood: Do you feel, as a result of this, that the hands become callous to the other members of the Body?

Señor Hand: Sí, señor. In fact, there are some Hands that say if things don't improve, they're going to get rough!

Brother Hood: That would be disastrous! Who do you think are the most important part in the Body of Christ?

Señor Hand: Oh, most definitely the hands! We feel that we have a great deal of common sense . . . we grasp things easily.

Mr. Foot:	How can you say something like that!
Brother Hood:	Mr. Foot!! Control yourself! This man is my guest and you have had your turn to speak! Señor Hand, I am so sorry!
Señor Hand:	It is all right, Hermano Hood.
Brother Hood:	Thank you for your enlightening remarks, Señor Hand. And now, may I introduce our next guest? From Canterbury-on-Avon, Worchestershire, England, Rector of the Q-tip Anglican Church, bring him on with a big hand, Reverand Ear! (Applause) Good evening, Reverand, and welcome to the Brotherhood Hour.
Rev. Ear:	What did you say? I didn't hear you.
Brother Hood:	I said welcome to the Brotherhood Hour!
Rev. Ear:	Oh! I'm sorry! Yes, it is good to be here.
Brother Hood:	Rev. Ear, you have just written a book, entitled *A History of Ears Within the Body of Christ,* published by the Earwax Press. In the book you mention, and I quote, "As a result of spiritual and social forces, Ears have become the greatest contributors to the Body of Christ." Why do you say that?
Rev. Ear:	Well, I feel that Ears, as a group, have gained superiority in that they are good listeners. We are indispensible to the Body.
Mr. Foot:	And you call yourself a minister?! That's a laugh!!
Rev. Ear:	What did he say?
Brother Hood:	Please sit down, Mr. Foot! Rev. Ear, what other contributions have the Ears made?
Rev. Ear:	We have been experimenting with musical instruments and have developed a new one for worship services. It's called an ear drum.
Brother Hood:	That sounds very interesting. Do you feel that the rest of the Body is deaf to these contributions?
Rev. Ear:	They are deaf only because they want to be. I believe this is because they are jealous.
Brother Hood:	Thank you Rev. Ear for your remarks. I'd like to discuss your book with you further, but I must bring on our next guest. Please welcome Mr. Eye from

	Bloodshot Hills near Lake Wawanunu, Minnesota. (Applause) Welcome to our program, Mr. Eye.
Mr. Eye:	Thank you, Brother Hood. I'm so glad to be here. My wife thought that I didn't have the nerve to appear on national television.
Brother Hood:	I guess you'd call that optic nerve! Seriously though, Mr. Eye, we are discussing Who or What is the Body of Christ. In general, how do the Eyes see the Body of Christ?
Mr. Eye:	We believe the "Eyes" have it!
Brother Hood:	Why do you say that?
Mr. Eye:	Because of our great scholastic standing. We have many pupils enrolled in our schools, you know. Due to our immense contribution to academia, we feel that we are indeed the most important part of the Body of Christ.
Mr. Foot:	That's it!! I've had it!! I'm not going to listen to any more of this garbage.
Rev. Ear:	I say, calm down old boy!
Mr. Foot:	You wanna take it outside, Parson?
Señor Hand:	You are nothing but a bully, señor!
Mr. Foot:	Take that! (Hits him)
Brother Hood:	Please, Mr. Foot . . . (Mr. Foot hits him too)

(A rumble occurs between all the guests. Brother Hood scrambles to his feet. He speaks while the rumble continues.)

Brother Hood:	Well that's our show for tonight. We hope you enjoyed it. Tune in next week when we will be discussing the Baptism of the Holy Spirit.

(Contributed by Steve Waters & Bruce Burkholder, Hershey, Pa.)

CHRISTMAS TREE GIFTS

This strategy is designed to help young people to examine the values expressed in giving and receiving gifts, and is obviously most appropriate during the Christmas season. Print up copies of the Christmas Tree drawing (shown below) on letter size paper so that everyone will have one. Second best would be to have the kids just draw a reasonable facsimile.

Each person should then "trim" his or her tree with symbolic drawings or words according to the instructions below:

1. On the "banner" around the tree, write a Christmas message that you would like to give to the world.
2. In space two, draw the best gift you ever got at Christmas - something so special that it is a high point in your Christmas memories.
3. Next, draw the gift that you would like to receive this Christmas more than anything else. You don't have to be realistic here - it can be anything.
4. Draw a gift that you gave to someone else that was especially appropriate and appreciated.
5. Draw the gift that you would bring to the manger. (Remember the wise men?) Let your gift say something about how you see Christ and your relationship to Him.
6. Symbolize some of the gifts that God has given to you in the sixth space.
7. At the base of the tree, write out some of the feelings that this exercise may have stirred up. What is the purpose of giving? Why do we give at Christmas? Do you feel uncomfortable about some of the drawings you have made? Do you feel pride? Thanksgiving?

After the exercise, discussion or voluntary sharing may be appropriate. You may want to divide into small groups and allow each person to share what he or she drew or wrote on their Christmas Tree. (Contributed by John Boller, Jr., San Diego, California)

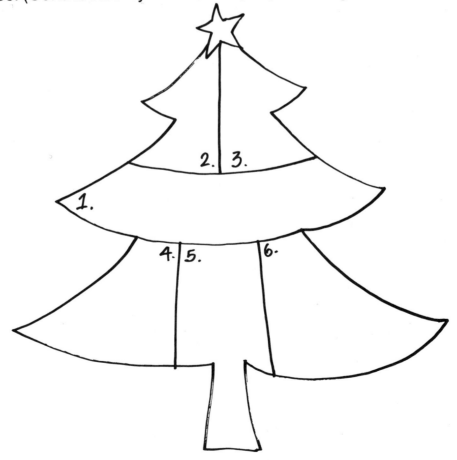

CHUG-A-LUG

If your group is like most, they like to do musical activities, except they are tired of guitars and things that only a few can participate in. A jug band is a great way to relieve this frustration and have fun at the same time. Even the least talented member of your group can beat two wooden blocks together. A jug band is not limited to jugs, you can be as creative as you want by turning anything (jars, pans, washboards, etc.) into instruments. (Contributed by Marja Coons, Albuquerque, New Mexico)

COMMERCIAL CHURCH

This can be a very useful discussion starter on the subject of the church in modern society and its use or misuse of media. First of all, have each person list all of the characteristics of the church. Then on a blackboard or overhead projector, combine everyone's lists into one master list. Divide into small groups and have each group choose what they think are the most important characteristics (important to those who know nothing about the church). Have each group spend an evening writing radio, newspaper, and television advertising built around those characteristics.

Have each group present its advertising package to the whole group for discussion and evaluation. You might want to go a step further by voting on the "best" advertising package and present it to a group of adults in the church for interaction between both age groups. (Contributed by Marja Coons, Albuquerque, New Mexico)

COST OF DISCIPLESHIP

The following is a list of five significant New Testament scriptures dealing with the meaning of discipleship. The questions under each passage are excellent discussion starters to help your group focus on the main issue of each passage. This exercise is most effective if done with small groups of 5-10.

Pass out a copy of the questions below and have each young person circle what they consider to be the *best* answer for each question. There is also a space to write an answer if they feel none of the others is sufficient.

Read Luke 9:23-25
1. To me "taking up my cross daily" means:
    a. Do things I hate to do
    b. Facing death
    c. Being teased because I am a Christian
    d. Accepting anything that God desires of me as part of his plan for my life.
    e. None of the above
    f. _____

74

2. Denying self means denying anything which would prevent complete commitment to Christ. For me this has meant:
   a. Nothing as I haven't made this type of commitment yet.
   b. Nothing as I don't understand how to do this.
   c. Attempting to quit being lazy in my job at home, school, work, or church.
   d. To quit trying so hard and let Christ take over.
   e. Give up my favorite T.V. show on Thursday to come to Sr. hi. meeting.
   f. _____

Read John 17:13-24
1. Being "one" here means:
   a. Doing things together.
   b. Never disagree. Always accept the others viewpoint.
   c. Learning to love, share, and to work closely with each other.
   d. _____
2. This "oneness" can be achieved by:
   a. Denying self — and sharing our gut feelings with each other.
   b. Stop disagreeing with others.
   c. Getting to know others in the group better.
   d. It's too difficult, so I won't try.
   e. _____

Read I John 3:23,24; John 13:34-35.
1. This type of love means:
   a. Action — Must share myself with others.
   b. Attitude — finding the good in other people.
   c. Loving them enough to help them with their problems.
   d. All the above
   e. _____
2. A "personal relationship with God" to me means:
   a. Asking Christ to forgive me.
   b. Having visions of God talking to me.
   c. Won't really happen till heaven
   d. Accepting Christ as my best friend.
   e. _____

Read I Corinthians 15:49 and I John 3:2
1. Becoming like Christ means
   a. Sinning less and less
   b. Learning to love as Christ loved.
   c. Learning to minister for Christ better
   d. Growing in knowledge of God and the Bible.
   e. _____

(Contributed by Phillip Ladd, Coon Rapids, Minnesota)

CREATION MEDITATION

Meditation is difficult for all of us and this one is excellent for those who are new at it. Ask the kids to sit on the floor in a circle with legs crossed. Place a cup of soil and a cup of water before each participant. Ask them to note where the water and soil have been placed and then have them close their eyes and relax. Explain that you will be reading selected verses from Genesis and that you want them to use their imaginations in giving God thanks for his creation.

LEADER:

Read Gen. 1: 1 & 3 and say: "Thank God for light. What if you lived in darkness? Picture the face of someone that you dearly love — a friend, a parent, a boyfriend or girlfriend. Now let that face melt away into darkness. What if you lived in darkness? Thank God for light!" (Keep your eyes closed).

Read Gen. 1:6 and say: "Do you take water for granted? What if we should run out of it? Taste a few drops. Keep it in your mouth. Appreciate it for a moment. All of life depends upon it. Thank God for water."

Read Gen. 1:9 and say: "Do you take soil for granted? Reach out now and touch it. Rub it between your fingers. Smell it. What if we should pollute all of it? Could we exist? Thank God for soil!"

Read Gen. 1:14 and say: "What if the seasons never changed? What if it were always winter? Picture your yard at home with no flowers, no leaves on the trees, no green bushes — not just for a few months out of the year, but for the whole year long. Thank God for the seasons."

Say: "Lay back now and completely relax while we continue to thank God for his creation" (it is good to change positions for the sake of comfort and relaxation,) Read Gen. 1:20 and Say: "Thank God for birds. They teach us to soar. Picture yourself as a gliding seagull. You are flying over the ocean. You approach the shoreline and see the water lapping the shore. Now fly away and see whatever you want to see. Right now, in your imagination. Fly as high or as far as you would like. Come back to land now. You are again walking upon the shore. Thank God for birds."

Read Gen. 1:24 and say "Now picture yourself as some kind of animal. Any kind. What kind of animal are you? Where do you live? What is it like there today? What are you doing? Thank God for animals."

Read Gen. 1:26-27 and say: "Thank God for you. Do you appreciate yourself? Keep your eyes closed. Run your hand through your hair. Is it fine or coarse? Now touch your ear. Run your finger along its edge. Feel its shape. Now without opening your eyes, put your hand in front of your face. Try to remember what it looks like. Try to picture how many lines run across your palm. Try to feel how the veins run across the backside of your hand. Now open your eyes and look closely at your hand, and thank God for you."

Let us pray: Dear God, we thank you for all your creation. Help us never to take it for granted. In Jesus' name. Amen.

NOTE: All questions above are rhetorical. Each section should be read slowly, and quietly, with pauses after each question. The entire meditation should be adapted to one's geographical area. (Contributed by Douglas Iben, Edmonds, Washington)

CREATIVE TEACHING WITH THE PSALMS

The Psalms can be effectively used for teaching the concepts of prayer and petition, praise and thanksgiving. They are also helpful in communicating to a group the grappling of individuals and the community of the faithful with the emotions of grief, despair, sorrow, love, hate, joy, and excitement. Below are two types of psalms which can be utilized along these lines.

I. COMPLAINT PSALMS
  A. Information
    1. Intention of complaints: to petition God to change or alleviate the situation
    2. Examples of the two types:

        Individual — Ps. 5, 6, 13, 22, 28, 38, 43, 54, 61
        Community — Ps. 44, 74, 80, 83, 94

    3. Historical situations of the complaint: I Samuel 1:9-18; I Samuel 7; Jeremiah 14:1-9, 17-22.
    4. Situations of the complainers: illness; defeat, persecution; oppression, discouragement, physical needs (child-bearing, rain, food, etc.), sin.
    5. Constituent parts of all complaints: a) invocation; b) complaint; c) prayer for change. In some psalms there are two additional parts: d) motivation for God to help; and e) assurance of God's hearing.

        An Example: Psalm 22
          I. Invocation *(My God, my God)* 22:1a
          II. Complaint *(I cry . . . you do not answer)* 1b-2
          III. Motivation *(Our fathers trusted you)* 3-5
          IV. Complaint *(Scorned by men)* 6-8
          V. Motivation *(You have been my God)* 9-10
          VI. Supplication *(Be not far from me)* 11
          VII. Complaint *(Many bulls encompass me)* 12-18
          VIII. Supplication *(Be not far off)* 19-21
          IX. Assurance of hearing and praise *(He has heard, when he cried)* . 22-31

B. Group Activity
1. Have the group go over the parts of a complaint psalm; then have them identify the different parts of a particular psalm into its invocation, complaint and supplication (and motivation and assurance of hearing if applicable).
2. Have them identify the different emotions and attitudes (despair, anger, sorrow, fear, dread, disgust, etc.) and why the writer had reason to feel this way. Have them examine what the writer wanted God to do about his situation.
3. Have the group as a whole or in small groups share experiences in which they have had similar feelings and attitudes. Ask them how they responded to the situation, i.e., praying, asking for advice from friends, self-pity, etc.
4. Have each person in the group take ten to fifteen minutes to write a psalm of their own, and then share some of them with the whole group. It can be either a complaint of the community, i.e. one that effects your whole group, or Christians as a whole, or an individual complaint.

II. PSALMS OF PRAISE
A. Information
1. Intention of a hymn of praise: to praise God for who He is and what He has done; and to call others to praise Him.
2. Examples:
   Pss. 19:1-6, 29, 30, 33, 47, 48, 65, 66, 92, 93, 95, 96, 97, 98, 100, 101, 103, 111, 113, 145-150.
3. Situations of the writers: Experiences of deliverance from sickness, distress; thankfulness for God's helping the needy, for the gift of children, for the righteous, for His love, for His justice and mercy; and praise for creation, ad infinitum.
4. There is no specific form or any particular arrangement of the content in a psalm of praise.
B. Group Activity
1. Have the group identify the different moods of the psalm; joy, praise, relief, thanks, etc., and the reasons the writer felt this way.
2. Have the group as a whole or in small groups share times when they have been thankful, or wanted to praise God. Ask them to share what they did about it, i.e. shouted, prayed, told a friend, etc.
3. Have each one in the group write their own psalm of praise, and then read some of them to the whole group. Remind the group that the criteria of a complaint or praise psalm is not first and foremost that it be wonderful poetry, but that it first of all is addressed to God from the heart, and not contrived. The results of really putting some

thought into this are quite rewarding, and the group can both come to some insights about the psalms, themselves, and each other.
(Contributed by K.C. Hanson, Placentia, Calif.)

DEAR ABBY

Occasionally young people encounter situations in which they would like advice in a Christian atmosphere, but are embarrassed about bringing their questions openly before their peers. This suggestion might provide an answer to the problem.

Give each young person a piece of paper and a pencil and instruct them to write down in letter form, some problem that is bothering them. This could be a family problem, a problem at school, a problem that requires Christian advice. The letter should be addressed to "Dear Abby" to give the feeling of appealing to some uninvolved source. These would be signed with an anonymous signature ("Concerned" or "Wants to Know"). The letters would then be collected and read to the group for their advice.

This not only gives the group a chance to help (who knows, their advice might be better than an adult's), but also gives them a chance to see that others are having problems very similar to their own. (Contributed by Larry Bennett, Mitchell, Indiana)

DEATH FANTASY

Here is a list of questions that have been used effectively to help young people express their feelings about death and dying. By using fantasy or "make believe," young people very often surface their hidden or sub-conscious feelings about death. This can be either a written quiz or a discussion.

1. How do you most frequently see yourself dying?
2. Who died the way you expect to die?
3. What, to you, would be the worst possible way to die? The best possible way?
4. What habits or characteristics of your life may influence the way you die?
5. When do you think you will die? When would you like to die?
6. What is your dominant attitude or feeling about death (defiance, acceptance, fear, longing, curiosity, avoidance)?
7. Imagine you died yesterday...what would things be like?
8. What are you doing now to help lengthen your life? Shorten your life?
9. What do you want to accomplish before you die?

Other optional questions:

1. Describe how you reacted to the death of someone you knew. Did you feel anger, fear, relief, sorrow, pity, frustration?
2. Whose death would bring you the greatest sorrow? The greatest pleasure?
3. Who would care the most if you died? What would they do?
4. Describe your funeral.
5. What will you have inscribed on your tombstone?

(Contributed by John Boller, Jr., San Diego, California)

DEATH MYTHS

In the world of myth, death is usually considered an unnatural event, a strangeness in need of an explanation. Here is an African myth that tells why death came into the world:

> "Formerly men had no fire but ate all their food raw. At that time they did not need to die for when they became old God made them young again. One day they decided to beg God for fire. They sent a messenger to God to convey their request. God replied to the messenger that he would give them fire if he was prepared to die. The man took the fire from God, but ever since then all men must die."

Now have each person make up their own myth about why we must die and then share them with the group. Discussion can follow. See "Run for Your Life" and "Death Fantasy" also in this chapter. (Contributed by John Boller, Jr., San Diego, California)

DIAL-AN-INSPIRATION

Here's an effective way to give kids the opportunity to verbalize their faith creatively and to share it with others in the church. Distribute paper and pencils to each person and ask them to write a 60 second inspirational message that could be given out over the telephone. Explain that they must consider the caller's possible emotional state (loneliness, depression, discouragement, confusion, etc.) as they write their messages. Their first line should read something like "Thank you for calling Dial-an-Inspiration...." and then their message.

After they have put some ideas down, tell them that next week during youth group meeting, they will get a chance to read them. This gives them a week to polish them up at home, and also gives you a week to announce it to the church or put it in the church bulletin. Notify the congregation that next week during the time that the youth group meets, they are to call the church. If the line is busy, try again. (If the church has an auxiliary number, you might use that one so the church's main line won't be tied up.) Then have the kids line up outside the office (where the phone is) or give them numbers, and send them in one at a time to sit by the phone and wait until it rings. This avoids any fear or embarrassment by having the other kids around listening in. After each person has a chance to read his message to the caller, he or she then goes to the end of the line, or waits until his or her number is called again. (Contributed by Len Carlson, Hopkins, Minnesota)

DO IT YOURSELF CHRISTMAS CARDS

Why not have your group make their own Christmas cards this year? Use a simple block printing technique, or collage on construction paper, or if your group is really talented, get into silk screening *(See Ideas Number Two)*. Here are some ways to use them.

1. If you can make enough, package them in bundles of five or ten and sell them to members of your congreation as a fund- raiser to buy presents for needy children.
2. Ask your pastor for a list of the shut ins in your congregation and assign each young person one or two names to send a card to.
3. Send cards to every patient in a nearby nursing home or the pediatric ward of your local hospital.

(Contributed by Marja Coons, Albuquerque, New Mexico)

EASTER ON THE NETWORK NEWS

The following is an outline for a youth sunrise service or Easter program that can be conducted by the youth for the entire church body. Assign the character parts to various members of the youth group. The characters then study the scene(s) they are to participate in, study the appropriate Scripture, and then work out the necessary dialogue, based on the facts in the Scripture. It is best to rehearse the entire service a few times before its presentation, and it can be refined during the rehearsal process. A songleader is needed to involve the congregation in singing between the "newscasts." Some of the music, however, can be performed as solos, duets, or instrumentals.

Props do not have to be elaborate. People may use their imaginations. The dialogue is the most important part. You will want to set up a table and chair situation for the "anchorman", similar to a news broadcast on television. Since the idea is to recreate the Easter story as a current event, contemporary dress can be worn by everyone involved. The reporters who are "on-the-scene" may appear in various places around the room or platform. Since the anchorman sets each scene, props are not necessary, but your own creativity and resources can dictate this.

The service may be introduced with remarks similar to these: "This morning's commemoration of this historical event is not one that fits with the usual sunrise service. But we trust that it will be used by God's Spirit to help you celebrate this joyous event. What we celebrate today happened many years ago...but what if these events had taken place today? What if God had chosen to reveal himself in Christ to our generation? How might these events have been reported through the news media? That is the setting for this service."

Scene Synopsis:

I. *T.V. Newsroom and Garden of Gethsemane:* Anchorman giving evening news on Thursday evening. Among other news items, he reports that..."Jesus Christ has just been arrested by a Roman battalion. For a report we go to the Garden of Gethsemane." There the reporter on the scene pieces together the story of the betrayal and arrest of Christ (which has just taken place). (Matthew 26:47-57) He reports back to the anchorman. (Suggested Songs: *Go To Dark Gethsemane, Tis Midnight,* and *On Olive's Brow*)

2. *T.V. Newsroom and Trial "Courtyard": (Late Thursday night)* Anchorman breaks in with a late breaking news development on the trial of Christ. "For a report we go to the High Priest's chambers." Reporter standing in the courtyard gives a report on the trial. (Matthew 26:59-68) Reporter then spots Peter and interviews him. (Matthew 26:69-75) He reports back to the anchorman with the trial still in progress. (Suggested Song: *Bold Peter Denied His Lord*)

3. *T.V. Newsroom and Governor Pilate's Courtyard: (Friday morning)* Anchorman reports that the trial is over. Jesus has been condemned to die on the cross and they are leading him up the hill to Golgotha now. "For a report, we go to Governor Pilate where we have a reporter standing by." The reporter interviews Pilate concerning the trial, particularly his feelings. (Matthew 27:11-26) After interviewing Pilate, the reporter spots Barrabas, the criminal released in place of Christ. He interviews Barrabas.(Matthew 27:15-21) Then he reports back to the anchorman. The anchorman gives an update on Judas who betrayed Christ. (Matthew 27:3-5) (Suggested Song: *The Old Rugged Cross*)

4. *T.V. Newsroom and the crucifixion site: (Friday afternoon)* Anchorman reports that Christ is on the cross. He reports and comments on some of the strange events associated with the crucifixion. (Matthew 27:45-53) "For a report on the crucifixion, we go to Golgotha." The reporter gives a brief account of what happened. (Matthew 27:27-50) Then he interviews the centurion (27:54) and Mary Magdalene (27:55-56). (A little more

imagination is needed for these two interviews because of little Scriptural information.)

5. *T.V. Newsroom and Burial Site: (Saturday morning)* Anchorman reports that Christ's body has been taken down from the cross and bound in the tomb of Joseph of Arimathea.(Matthew 27:57-60) "For a report we go to the tomb site." Reporter interviews some soldiers who are busy at the entrance of the tomb. (Matthew 27:62-66) (Suggested Song: *Christ Arose*)

6. *T.V. Newsroom and Burial Site: (Sunday morning)* Anchorman reports a rumor that the tomb in which Christ was laid is empty. "For an accurate report we go to the tombsite where a reporter is standing by." He sums up what seems to be happening. Then he speaks with Mary, Mary Magdalene, Peter, and John standing in a group wondering what happened to the body of Christ. (Matthew 28:1-7, John 20:1-l0) He also speaks with the guards, huddled in another group. (Matthew 27:4, ll-l5) He reports back to the anchorman. As the anchorman is summarizing, another reporter cuts in with a report of two men who have seen and talked with Christ. (Luke (Luke 24:13-35) Almost immediately another reporter cuts in with a report from Mary Magdalene who has seen and talked with Christ. (John 20:11-18) (Suggested Song: *Christ the Lord Is Risen Today*)

7. Final commentary on the weekend's events by the anchorman. (Suggested Song: *Alleluia*)

(Contributed by Douglas Swank, Homewood, Illinois)

ENGLISH TEST

Below is a fun way to show kids how we often make judgments too hastily. Pass out copies of the following paragraph and have each person make the corrections as instructed. Most will blow it every time. When they are finished, follow up with a discussion on Matthew 7:1-6.

> Mark this paragraph into sentences using capitals at the beginning, periods at the end of sentences, and commas, etc. where needed. Once begun, DO NOT GO BACK and try to correct.
>
> He is a young man yet experienced in vice and wickedness he is never found in opposing the works of iniquity he takes delight in the downfall of his neighbors he never rejoices in the prosperity of his fellow-creatures he is always ready to assist in destroying the peace of society he takes no pleasure in serving the Lord he is uncommonly diligent in sowing discord among his friends and acquaintances he takes no pride in laboring to promote the cause of Christianity he has not been negligent in endeavoring to tear down the church he makes no effort to subdue his evil passions he strives hard to build up satan's kingdom he lends no aid to the support of the gospel among heathen he contributes largely to the devil he will never go to heaven he must go where he will receive his just reward.

Here is the way it should be corrected.

He is a young man, yet experienced. In vice and wickedness, he is never found. In opposing the works of iniquity, he takes delight. In the downfall of his neighbors, he never rejoices. In the prosperity of his fellow-creatures, he is always ready to assist. In destroying the peace of society, he takes no pleasure. In serving the Lord, he is uncommonly diligent. In sowing discord among his friends and acquaintances, he takes no pride. In laboring to promote the cause of Christianity, he has not been negligent. In endeavoring to tear down the church, he makes no effort. To subdue his evil passions, he strives hard. To build up satan's kingdom, he lends no aid. To the support of the gospel among heathen, he contributes largely. To the devil he will never go. To heaven he must go, where he will receive his just reward.

(Contributed by Ron Malin, Mt. Morris, Michigan)

ESTHER AND THE KING

The Old Testament book of Esther is one of the most fascinating stories of the Bible and is an excellent book for group study and discussion.

Have the group read through the entire book in one sitting. This normally takes about 20 minutes (if you read from a modern translation). Then discuss the following questions:

1. Esther never mentions the name of God. In spite of this, can you find evidence of God in Esther? (Have the group take a chapter at a time and point out places where they find God, such as verses 4:14 or 6:1-2. There are many more.)

2. Discuss the *advice* that was given to various people in the story. (Such as 1:16, 3:8, 4:13, 5:14, etc.) Which was good advice, which was bad? Who gives *you* advice?

3. Rank order the main characters in the story from best to worst. Who was the best person, who was the worst? (Give reasons why.) The main characters are (in alphabetical order):

   a. Ahasuerus, the King   e. Mordecai

   b. Esther   f. Vashti, the Queen

   c. Haman   g. Zeresh, Haman's wife

   d. Memucan (1:16)

4. If you could write a "moral to the story," what would it be?

Of course, there are other excellent questions that will come up in the study of Esther, but these will help towards good discussion.

Esther can also be written as a play and acted out for the church very effectively. The story contains interesting dialogue and characters, a good plot, suspense, and a bit of irony. Most of all it will help young people to gain more insights into and appreciation for the Old Testament.

EUTHANASIA ON TRIAL

This mock trial idea not only raises a very timely and difficult issue but allows the entire youth group to participate in the decision making process.

The setting is a trial or hearing on the issue of Euthanasia (this could also work with any other "sticky" issue). Part of the youth group is designated the jury, the rest are court room observers. Youth sponsors can be used as the lawyers to present the pro and con side of the issue to the jury. Youth group members can be chosen to represent family members in the three cases described. The youth minister or another sponsor plays the part of judge. (It is important that the "judge" acquaint himself thoroughly with the issue along with portions of Scripture that are applicable.)

The job of the lawyers is to present a convincing case for either the "pro" or "con" side of the issue using whatever sources they can find to prove their argument. They can also call witnesses (youth group members who represent family members in the cases described) to bolster their case. Of course, there should be opportunity for cross examination. After both cases have been presented and summary statements made, the jury adjourns for a matter of minutes to vote on the issues. The jury is *not* deciding on the pro and con of euthanasia, rather on Case A, B and C. The jury should then vote on each case and give the results to the judge who will read the results to the "courtroom". (There should be little or no discussion by the jury while deliberating. Save that for the discussion with the whole group later).

The entire group then discusses the decisions. The judge can then wrap up the discussion with some Biblical insights without telling the group the conclusions they should have reached. Let the young people go home and struggle with their decision themselves.

CASES FOR THE JURY TO CONSIDER:

A. Hortense is a severly retarded, 19 year old girl. She has control of her motor (muscular) faculties but seems to be around the age of 1 or 2 mentally. Through nearly 8 years of therapy, doctors and aides have taught her to button the buttons on her clothes. The method they used was much like the method a dog trainer would use to teach a dog tricks: stimulus-response. She *might* be able to be trained to hold down some extremely simple job on a factory production line, but it would take years to train her. Those years would take large amounts of money both from taxpayers and family, in addition it would take precious time from a doctor or psychiatrist who could be spending his time on someone who was more "promising". The family of this patient has asked that they be released from any legal holdings on Hortense, or if that is not possible, that she be mercifully put to death. The jury must decide.

B. Alex is a successful 47 year old business man. He went in to the doctor for a routine check-up and the doctor found a large lump in the middle of Alex's back that he didn't like the looks of. X-rays were taken and it was found to be cancer of some sort. A biopsy was done and the cancer was determined to be malignant. It was too far along to take out so radiation therapy was performed. That was unsuccessful and month later Alex is in the hospital in a coma. Doctors believe that he won't live past six months, but he could be given medication (morphine) to lessen the pain. He would have to remain in the Intensive Care Ward till death ($120/day) plus the family would have to bear the cost of doctors bills and medication totaling thousands of dollars. This family could bear the expense but they cannot bear to see the pain that Alex is in, and so ask the doctors to either 1) give Alex a lethal dose of morphine; or, 2) discontinue all medications and care and let him die naturally and hopefully quickly. The jury must decide.

C. A baby is born to John and Jane Doe. They have waited so long for a child and both eagerly await the time when they can go on home with their new arrival. The shape of the baby's head bothered a couple of the doctors and routine tests were run to test the baby's brain waves. It was found that during delivery the baby's skull contracted too tightly around the brain and the child suffered severe brain damage to the point that it will be a complete idiot mentally. The baby remained in intensive care while John and Jane went home to think the whole matter over. They are just a young couple, and have no way financially of putting the child in an institution. They decided to go to the doctor and ask if the child could be put out of its misery, and they would try to have another child. It was brought before the courts and the jury must decide.

LAWYER'S CASE AGAINST EUTHANASIA

1. Euthanasia could easily be misconstrued as a mere recommendation of suicide or of wholesale murder or aged or infirmed people.
2. How could a weak and/or unbalanced mind, incapable of weighing aright the conditions which may be held to render death more desirable than life, make this momentous decision?

Case-in point: One miraculous cure given a great deal of publicity was that of a clergyman's wife who, in a widely circulated letter, had begged for "scientific kindness" by her physicians to terminate her suffering and give her painless death. Many laymen supported her arguments, but the physicians ignored them and succeeded in restoring her health. She rejoiced that her pleas were disregarded.

3. What about the obstacles concerning practical applications in our modern society — who will determine who is to die and how.
4. If infants born with idiocy, retardation, or complete body disfigurement are put to death under a Euthanasia Law, this would lead to a degrading of morality, a new form of infanticide. In other words, belated abortion.
5. One alternative is segregation and special training instead of Euthanasia. For example, the feeble minded can be made actually useful, as many of them have considerable physical skill, and they seem to be happy under such conditions.
6. We should hold on to the value of the individual and the value of life at any cost.
7. Wouldn't a pro-euthanasia morality have a hard time dealing with incidences or mistakes and/or abuse?
8. What about the danger that legal machinery initially designed to kill those who are a pain to themselves may some day engulf those who are a pain to others?

LAWYER'S CASE FOR EUTHANASIA

1. What type of life would a baby have who was born mongoloid or a complete vegetable — the issue is "quality" of life, rather than "quantity".
2. Special segregation and training involves heavy expense of all sorts: emotional and economic.
3. A "carefully controlled system" of euthanasia would eliminate the most hopeless cases at once.
4. The quality of life of those around the incapacitated individual will be adversely affected if the individual is left to linger in pain.
5. There are those who are afflicted with incurable and painful diseases who want to die quickly. A law which tries to prevent such sufferers from achieving this quick death, and thereby forces other people who care for them to watch their pointless pain helplessly, is a very cruel law! In such cases the sufferer may be reduced to an obscene image of a human being, a lump of suffering flesh eased only by intervals of drugged stupor.
6. There should be a concern for human dignity, an unwillingness to let the animal pain disintegrate a person.
7. Suffering is evil. If it were not, why then do we expend so much

energy in trying to relieve it.

8. The goal of the Euthanasia society, "would permit an adult person of sound mind, whose life is ending with much suffering, to choose between an easy death and a hard one, and to obtain medical aid in implementing that choice".

(Contributed by Stephen Wing, Dodge City, Kansas)

THE EXECUTION

The following short play is good for use as a discussion starter or as a statement on the meaning of the Crucifixion. It requires two characters who have speaking parts (Calvinicus and Georgius) and any number of others who carry out the action as described in the column "Visual" below. Calvinicus and Georgius carry on their conversation totally oblivious to what is going on behind them.

VISUAL	AUDIO
Camera (or spotlight) on men eating lunch.	*Calvinicus:* Hi, George, What's new?
	Georgius: What d'ya mean? Nothing ever happens around here. Looks like another hot one. Nice day for camels, eh?
	C: (chuckles) Yeah, pass me an olive, will ya?
	G: Here you are, ya beggar. Why don't you get yourself a bowl and sit at the Jerusalem gate?
	C: Lay off, ok? It's been rough enough today out there in the fields. Look at these fingernails!
People start walking across behind the workmen.	G: Yeah, I know. The ground is so hard. Almost broke the yoke right off my ox.
	C: What's going on anyway? What's all this commotion about?
	G: Oh, just another execution. You know, one of those weird "prophets." Claim they got the answer to all the world's problems. Bein' executed along with two other criminals.
	C: Oh. He's the guy. Yeah, I heard about him. They say he's God or something. Some people say he did some kind of hocus pocus on some sick people.
A small cross is carried in and set to one side.	G: Yeah. These "prophets" are all the same. They supposedly fix a few legs and eyes and everyone goes ga-ga. Course, he's also charged with creating a disturbance, inciting a riot, and contempt of court. They never learn. If he really wants a following, he's gotta explain how come his God is so good at fixing legs and so bad at gettin' him outta jail. Uh . . . look . . . I gotta get back to the

house and start preparing for the feast tonight.

C: You know, George, just the other day I was telling the wife what a mess the world is in. On one hand you got those radical Zealots and Essenes walking around with the short hair and stuff, and on the other hand you got those phony loudmouthed pharisees running around blowing trumpets and prayin' in your ear. What are things coming to anyway?

G: I don't know, man. Why don't you ask Caesar?

C: I know this sounds weird, George, but sometimes I think if there is a God, I wish he'd do something radical about what's going' on down here. I mean, you know, he could always come down here and zap a few Romans. Then maybe something would happen.

A second small cross is brought in and set to the other side.

G: It'd be great' if anything would happen around here! Every day . . . out to the fields . . . plow, plow, plow . . . grab a quick lunch . . . back to work . . . crunch the grain . . . the same old grind. What kind of life is that?

C: It sure would be great if we could all go back to the good old days of sheepherding like the Waltonbergs.

G: Are you kidding? I wouldn't go back to sheep for nothin'. Progress, man, progress. Oh sure, it gets a little dusty in town with all the traffic, but this is where the action is. Of course, all this activity has made my wife nag a little more (if that's possible.)

C: I don't know, man. Seems like I just wake up, turn off my rooster, go to work, go home, blow out the lamp and go to bed. I wish there was something more. I'm beginning to wonder about all this religious stuff. I mean, if there is such a thing as God, why doesn't He just come down here and say, "Hi, folks. I'm God. How'd you like to see a few Romans made into pizza."

G: You ought to know by now, Cal, baby, religion is all a bunch of myths and stuff. Well, see you around.

A third large cross is slowly brought in.

C: Ok, George, see you later.

G: (Sarcastically) Yeah. By the way, Cal, if you bump into some guy that says, "Hi, I'm God," let me know . . . I'd like to meet him.

(Contributed by Larry Michaels, Grosse Point Woods, Michigan)

EXMAS IN ACREMA

Here's a great idea for Christmas that can either be read as a sermon, duplicated and discussed after everyone has read it, or even narrated while being acted out. Here are some questions for discussion that might be used:

1. If you could control Christmas, what would you change?
2. What would you consider a good way to keep Exmas and Crissmas from getting confused?
3. Do you think it would be best for the church just to cancel Christmas and celebrate Christ's birth some other time?
4. What is the best way to get people to understand the real meaning of Christmas? Advertising, Church pageants, or what?

A Letter Home:

My travels have taken me to a strange and wonderful country called Acrema. It is a land of many contradictions. It has high mountains yet flat plains. It has vast open spaces, yet cities crammed with people. It even has a holiday filled with contradictions—a holiday called Exmas.

Preparations for this festival last for over fifty days and yet on the one day of what is supposed to be celebration, there is more quiet than merriment. It is difficult to determine whether the holiday itself or the preparation for it is the reason for the season. The preparations are very strange. They begin when people purchase tremendous quantities of cardboard cards with pictures and messages upon them. The pictures are of various subjects. Some portray snow scenes, some depict fireplaces; some have quite a modern tone; some are pictures of the way Acremans believe their ancestors lived. The pictures convey no central theme. The messages inside the cards are equally nebulous. Most often they say, "Seasons Greetings", which could be said at any time of the year. It is very difficult to say what the whole Exmas Season is supposed to represent. Some have proposed that its name be changed to "Great Religious Leader's Day" and that it be celebrated the fourth Monday of December. Although the cards are seemingly innocuous and vague, they cause untold suffering. The Acreman keeps long lists, which are called Exmas Card Lists. A card is sent to everyone on the list. Great care is taken that no one on the list is missed. Apparently some curse is associated with neglecting someone. When the task is finally finished and the cards are mailed, the Acreman sighs with relief and gives thanks to the gods that the task is over for one more year. All is peaceful then, as the Acreman receives cards which his friends have mailed him, unless he receives one from someone to whom he did not send an Exmas Card. Then there is much wailing and cursing of the gods as the Acreman pulls on his overcoat and boots, drives through unspeakably crowded streets to the equally crowded marketplace and mail the Exmas card that was forgotten.

An equally strange custom is the purchase of Exmas Gifts. This is a very difficult procedure. Another list is made after which an elaborate guessing game begins. Every citizen has to guess the value of the gift which every friend will send him so that he may send one of equal value, whether he can afford it or not. And they buy as gifts for one another such things as no man ever bought for himself. For the sellers, understanding the custom, put forth all kinds of trumpery, and whatever, being useless and ridiculous, they have been unable to sell throughout the year, they now sell as an Exmas Gift. And although the Acremans profess to lack sufficient necessary things, such as metal, leather, wood, and paper, yet an incredible quantity of these things is being wasted every year, being made into gifts. When the gifts are exchanged, gratitude must be profusely expressed. Though the gifts are often useless and the gratitude is largely insincere, the Acreman must manufacture a show of their delight. He even has to grind out written notes to express his unfelt "gratitude". The sellers of the gifts, as well as the buyers, become exceedingly exhausted from the strain of the crowds and traffic. They are frantic in their attempts to finish everything on time and yet are in constant need of stopping and resting. This frenzied state, in their barbaric language, is known as the Exmas Rush. The people become pale and weary so that any stranger visiting Acrema at this time of the year would suppose that some great calamity had befallen the land. When the day of the festival arrives , the Acremans, except those with young children, sleep until noon, being worn out from the Exmas Rush and the excesses of the Exmas Parties. In the evening of Exmas Day, they eat five times what they usually eat. The next day heads and stomachs are greatly distressed from the eating and spirits consumed in excess.

The motivation for this strange behaviour is most confusing to our best scholars. The motivation could not possibly be merriment, for most Acremans seem more weary than joyful. Our best explanation is that their motivation must have its source in their pagan worship. Two deities seem particularly popular at this time. One is a weak, comical deity, represented by a man in a red suit and a long white beard. He seems to be a harmless totem of a worship of materialism. Only small children take him seriously. Adults usually greet this totem with a condescending smile.

The other object of worship centers around a very interesting contest of deities called bowls. Constant reference is made where ever Acremans gather to Super Bowls, Orange Bowls, Rose Bowls, Sugar Bowls, etc. It is probably named after the Bowl-shaped headgear worn by the participants. Each deity is represented by some fierce animal, i.e., Bears, Lions, Rams, Falcons, etc. At the exact time coinciding with the Exmas Rush, these deities have annual contests to determine supremacy. At least weekly, the spiritual leaders of the households gather in large numbers at the actual site of the contest. Those unable to make the pilgrimage to the contest worship in front of family alters or receiving sets in their homes, urging their favorite deity on to victory. Hecataeus, a second rate scholar, believes that these are not worship services, but only games that the people are playing. But no real scholar agrees with him. These contests are taken much too seriously to be mere games. Their statistics are chronicled much too thoroughly and remembered much too completely.

My opinion, which I share with many scholars, is that perhaps there is a connection between the worship of these deities and the annual ritual called the Exmas Rush. Perhaps the Exmas Rush is a type of Self-fadulation the Acremans believe their deities require of them. Why else would the people punish themselves so? If it is not to help their deities, the Exmas Rush just doesn't make sense.

There is another group in Acrema, almost too small to be mentioned at all, that celebrate a completely different festival at this time of the year. They call their celebration Crissmas.

The celebration centers around an ancient story about a baby that was born of very special birth many, many years ago. The story has it that there were signs in the heavens proclaiming this baby's birth. This unusual baby grew into an extraordinary man. The story has it that this man could walk on water. He could heal the sick. He could open the eyes of the blind and raise the dead. His life was absolutely perfect. Many said he was the Son of some God which they claimed was the only God. His life was cut short by execution. He was pronounced dead and buried. Those who believe in this person say that he came back from the dead and that he was reborn and went into the heavens. The believers in this occurance say that this person will come back again to judge the world. His followers claim that only those who believe in this will be forgiven.

So every Crissmas they remember again the birth of this One who is their "saviour". They continue to retell the story of his birth. They use figures of his mother, of a baby born in a stable and other helps in remembering his birth. They gather together on the eve of his birth date to sing and praise him. They light candles and say that He is the Truth that came into the world as a small light and now illuminates the whole world in his truth. These people call themselves Crisstians, I assume after this beautiful holiday.

I talked to the priest of one of these groups and asked him why they celebrate Crissmas on the same day as Exmas. It seemed terribly confusing to me. He said the date of Crissmas had long ago been established and had hoped that more Acremans would celebrate it as his group did, or that God would put it in their minds to celebrate Exmas on some other day or not at all. For Exmas and the Rush distracts the minds of even the few from sacred things. He was glad that men make merry at Crissmas, but in Exmas there is no merriment left. And when I asked why Acremans endured the rush, he replied, "It is, O Stranger, a racket". Using the words (I suppose) of some ancient oracle and speaking unintelligibly to me (for the racket is an instrument which the barbarians use in a game called tennis.)

Hecataeus, in his usual way of oversimplifying the facts, has formulated a hypothesis that Crissmas and Exmas are the same. This is utterly impossible. First of all, the pictures stamped on the Exmas Cards have nothing to do with the sacred story which the priests tell. Secondly, although most Acremans don't believe the religion of the few, they still send gifts and cards and participate in the Rush. It is unlikely that anyone would suffer so greatly for a God they did not know. Hecataeus's hypothesis also fails to account for the central event of the Exmas season—the Bowls—the contests of the deities for supremacy. Something as important as the Bowls would not be allowed to continue if the people were trying to remember their God. No, my theory ties it all together, except those who celebrate Crissmas. They are the strange ones. I have no idea where their story could have originated—unless it actually did happen.

(Contributed by Bill Serjak, Sylva, North Carolina)

FACE TO FACE

This game is great for giving people a non-threatening way to communicate what they believe. It is also great for helping people discover how well they know each other. The game is played by two, three, or four people with a regular deck of playing cards. Each player receives cards of the same suit, except the jack. Jacks, jokers, and whites are not used. The players sit face to face and the first player says a sentence expressing an attitude about something. These statements may describe *emotions*, for example "I feel fine when I am alone", *opinions* like "I am against capital punishment", *reactions* like "I blush when someone praises me", *tastes or preferences* such as "I like working out of doors", *values*, like "I feel it's more important to have a good reputation than to be rich" or *beliefs*, such as "I believe in reincarnation". Each player indicates his position on the statement made by choosing a card between (the ace serves as one) and ten. He or she chooses the card from one to ten on this basis:

1 indicates:	total disagreement
2 or 3 indicates:	strong disagreement
4 or 5 indicates:	slight disagreement
6 or 7 indicates:	slight agreement
8 or 9 indicates:	strong agreement
10 indicates:	total agreement

The player(s) then place the cards they have chosen down to their left. For the same statement, each player chooses a card which corresponds to the position taken by the other person, that is, the card he/she thinks the other player had chosen. The player places this second card face down to his/her right. The other player does the same thing: he/she places the "me" card to the left and the "you" card to the right. The players then turn over the cards, taking care not to reverse their positions.

Each player counts his points by noting the difference between the value of the right hand card (the one by which he describes his partner's position and the card his/her partner has placed before this card, namely his partner's left hand card. For example, let's say John and Louise are playing FACE TO FACE: John places a 9 to his right, thinking that Louise strongly agrees with the statement just said. Louise, however, has rated her own position with a 5. John's score is 4. Meanwhile, Louise has placed an 8 on her right to indicate what, in her estimation is John's position on the statement. John has rated himself with a 7. So, the score for Louise is 1.

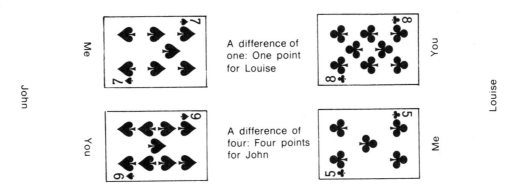

A difference of one: One point for Louise

A difference of four: Four points for John

The players note their scores, take back their cards and the next player makes a statement. Once again, each player lays down two cards as described above. Points are counted again and the first person or couple to obtain a score of 50 or 100 points loses the game.

If a player does not want to reveal his/her position on the statement given or to guess the position of his or her partner, he/she puts down a king or queen. The score for that player is then the highest of all other scores on the table for that particular round.

NOTE: If there are three players: one person makes a statement and the two others play FACE TO FACE, placing their cards and noting their scores. Then the next person makes a statement and the other two play FACE TO FACE, etc. If there are four players: the two people playing FACE TO FACE add up their points. This couple plays "against" the other couple. (Contributed by John Boller, San Diego, California)

FAKE FIT

Clue in two of your kids before a meeting to stage a confrontation. During the first part of the meeting one of the kids begins needling the other one. (Remind him/her not to overact.) Finally, the one being needled "blows up" and causes a scene making statements like "you're all a bunch of phonies, you don't act like Christians. My friends that aren't Christians treat me better than you do, etc." And walks out.

After the person leaves, attempt to go on with the meeting for a few minutes, watching the reactions of the group. Then explain that the little blow-up was a put-on and discuss what happened, what each person's reaction was and what they thought of the remarks made by the person who walked out. (Contributed by James Tishim, Des Moines, Iowa)

FAMILY PICTURES

Here is an idea that is useful for providing a sense of "belonging" in the youth group and also is a practical way of dividing up the kids for classes, activities, work projects and the like. The entire youth group is divided into "families" - groups of between eight and twelve kids each. Each family has a spiritual "mom and dad" (youth sponsors) and a family name. These families can be divided up according to age groups, schools, geographical locations (where they live), or any other way you choose. To help solidify these "families," have family pictures taken, and allow each family to dress up in a theme of their choice. They can dress up in old fashioned clothes, formal attire, hillbilly outfits, army fatigues, athletic gear, or whatever they choose. The pictures can then be used in the church paper, for printing youth group postcards, or simply for display on the youth bulletin board. (Contributed by Bob Leive, Lexington, Kentucky)

FOTO-MATCH

Hang up twenty or so photos of people (all kinds...old, young, black, attractive, ugly, fat, slim, wealthy, poor, etc.). The first week the pictures are displayed, have the kids write descriptions of each person based on what they see in the picture. Collect them all and during the following week, combine all the individual descriptions into a concise paragraph which accurately reflects the group consensus. Attach the descriptions to each picture for the next meeting. Have the students look at the photos with descriptions carefully (make sure they are numbered) and then answer the following questions:

1. Choose five people you would want to travel with for one year. Why?
2. Is there any one person you would not want anything to do with? Why?
3. Who, if any, would you be willing to marry?

94

4. Who, if any, would you worship with?
5. Which person do you think you could really like? Why?
6. If only five others and yourself were allowed to live and the others executed, which five would stay with you? Why?

You could have your group go through the questions again and decide how their parents would respond. And, of course, you can easily come up with other questions equally as good as these. (Adapted from an idea contributed by Pat Cox, Rochester, Illinois)

FOUR WORLDS

Four Worlds Exercise is an excellent simulation game on the world-wide hunger problem. It can be used effectively with senior highs on up.

Divide your youth at random into four groups. Each group gathers around a table in your youth room, and each selects a secretary. The secretary remains seated at the table throughout the exercise. As the exercise begins, the leader passes out to each group a certain number of 3 x 5 cards pre-cut from different colored construction paper. Any colors will do. The number of cards each group receives is as follows:

	GROUP #1	GROUP #2	GROUP #3	GROUP #4
YELLOW CARDS	15	8	5	2
GREEN CARDS	15	7	13	2
RED CARDS	7	8	15	5

Although you do not explain this to the participants until the exercise is over, the four groups represent the four power blocks of the world. Group #1 represents the Western nations, Group #2 represents Soviet dominated countries, Group #3 represents Third World energy producing nations, and Group #4 represents the under-developed countries. Also unknown to the participants is the meaning of the colored cards. Yellow cards represent food supplies, green cards represent money, and red cards represent natural resources (oil, gas, etc.). The number of cards given to each group is an estimate of the relative food, financial and natural resources of these various categories of countries. Make sure you don't explain this until *after* the exercise is over.

To begin, tell the participants that to complete their assignment, they need to acquire a certain number of cards, but not necessarily at the expense of other groups. Each team needs the following number of cards:

	GROUP #1	GROUP #2	GROUP #3	GROUP #4
YELLOW CARDS	10	10	7	10
RED CARDS	10	10	7	10

It is apparent from the two charts that some groups (such as Group #3) need very few cards, while others (such as Group #4) have a long way to go.

The leader then instructs all four groups that they have 20 minutes to negotiate with members of other groups for the cards they need. The ground rules (which should be written on a blackboard) are these:

1. Green cards may be traded for yellow or red cards.
2. Red cards may be traded for yellow ones, and yellows for reds.
3. Players may trade, beg or steal to get the cards their group needs, as long as decisions to do so are group decisions. No "lone ranger" diplomacy is allowed.
4. The group secretary holds all cards on the group table, in plain sight of other players.

(While giving these instructions, try to avoid competitive terms such as "team," "game," and "win." It isn't necessary for the four groups to compete against each other, though they usually do). The group members are then allowed to mix with each other and make deals. The leader keeps time, answers questions, and referees disputes. During the exercise, some players will probably figure out what's going on, while others will remain mystified.

When the time is up, ask each group in turn for their reactions. At this point, explain the meaning of the exercise. Give the group members feedback on some of the dynamics which went on. Notice especially if certain groups react much like the blocs of nations which they symbolize. Make sure to vent the good and bad feelings generated in the exercise.

After the exercise, continue with a discussion on world hunger. A filmstrip, such as the one produced by "Bread for the World" is helpful. Conclude by reading Matthew 25:31-40. (Contributed by Kenneth Baker, Roswell, New Mexico)

FREE ASSOCIATION GAME

This game can help your youth group get in touch with differing world views. For a warm-up, have each person write down the first word that comes to their mind after each of the following words is said:

Fish	Neck	God	Car
Pastor	Brother	Acne	Pit

After the list has been given, have the group share these "free-association" responses. Then divide the group into three small groups and give them the following instructions:

You have been divided into three groups each with a different identity The game we're playing depends on your individual responses as a member of your group. It is very important that you do not discuss your responses with any member of your group or with the members of other groups.

Now give each group their descriptions (see the descriptions below) and give them time to read and think about the character they are to be. Then have them free-associate the following words:

Sex	Dollar	Black	Death
Religion	Doctor	Pill	
Crime	Law	Health	
Future	Cheat	Home	

After everyone has responded to the complete list of words, compare each other's responses, first as individuals within each group and then as groups. This should lead to a very lively discussion.

Description For Group One: For a moment, forget your past and present life. Place yourself in the position of a person who has never known any life beyond that of the ghetto. With this in your mind, respond in one word associations to the list of words you are about to hear.

Description for Group Two: Think of yourself as being a parent. Consider the responsibilities entailed in making decisions that may affect your child for the rest of hisher life. How would you respond to the following list? (Use one word association answers.)

Description For Group Three: If you had to place yourself in the position of being a pusher. Your survival would be dependent upon your contact with street people. What would be your responses to the following words? (Use one word association answers.)

(Contributed by John Boller, Jr., San Diego, California)

GETTING OLD ON CASSETTE

Have several of your youth group take tape recorders with them when they visit an elderly person (grandparent, member of the church, someone at the park, or a stranger). Be sure to get the person's permission before turning on the tape, and then ask questions on topics where age would be invaluable for insight into a specific problem. Suggested topics: friendship, marriage, love, death, grief, meaning, patience. (Contributed by Keith Wise, Columbiana, Ohio)

GOSPEL ACCORDING TO DEAR ABBY

Select from assorted "Dear Abby" and "Ann Landers" columns, letters which reflect problems relevant to your youth group. Then read one of the letters to your group (Note: If a large group, give one letter to each small group) *without the columnist's reply.* Then discuss how they think Jesus would have answered the letter. After sufficient discussion, read the columnist's reply and compare her answer with Jesus' hypothetical answer. Discuss the differences, if any.

Read as many letters as time allows, skipping the ones that don't generate any interest. Another twist to this would be to have each individual write his/her response to the Dear Abby letter and then compare each other's responses. Then using each person's letter as a resource, have the group compile a group letter combining the best elements of each individual letter. (Contributed by Craig Boldman, Fairfield, Ohio)

Dear Abby

At 26, Her Life Has Become Meaningless

By ABIGAIL VAN BUREN

DEAR ABBY: Please help me. My laundry basket, piled high with unironed clothes, is staring me in the face. Dishes for the last two days are still unwashed and sitting in my sink. My apartment needs a good cleaning. I am overweight, yet I continue to stuff myself with more ice cream, cookies and sweets than I really want. I'm so depressed I could cry! I'm 26, divorced and rais- ~~g my 8-year-old son myself. I ~~ ~~ ~~ job, a nice ~~ ~~ ~~

I'm a terrific friend. I'm always doing something for others, but never do anything for myself. Maybe it's because I was raised by a mother who found fault with every- thing I did and a father who told me I would never amount to anything. Abby, am I going crazy or what? I've considered getting professional help, but I can't afford it. I've even considered committing suicide, but my son needs me. Thanks for listen- ing.

TIRED OF LIVING AT 26

living and feel like (bleep)." And it charges only what one can afford to pay. Please don't wait another day. You sound like a generous, warm- hearted, intelligent woman with some deep-rooted festering prob- lems to resolve. Please get the help you need, then write again and tell me of your progress. I care.

DEAR ABBY: A few years ago, I read that pigs make good pets. They're supposed to be cleaner, smarter and more easily trained tha dogs. I also heard they're gen- ~~ ~~dren ~~ ~~ make good

THE GOSPEL ACCORDING TO ME

Pass around to your youth group sheets of paper or cards with the words printed at the top THE GOSPEL ACCORDING TO _____. Have each person fill in their name and write their version of the story of Jesus. They should include their own beliefs about Jesus including areas where they have doubts as well. They can be as lengthy as they want. (Contributed by Bill Boggs, New Haven, Connecticut)

THE GREAT DONUT CRISIS
THE GREAT POPCORN CRISIS

Here are two very similar simulation games that can help your group deal with the problem of world hunger.

Divide your group into three nations and give them "Position Papers" describing the situation. Each group represents one of three mythical nations who are attending a food crisis summit conference. For the purposes of this game each nation's entire food supply is either donuts or popcorn.

Have each group read their position papers and then formulate a Position statement. Then the groups will meet together to hear each others statements. After the three opening statements, the floor is open for general statements on how the crisis can be averted. Following an adequate period of discussion, a de-briefing should follow discussing the real problem of hunger in the world.

INSTRUCTIONS

You represent one of three nations involved in this serious food shortage situation. Each group has ten minutes to perform the following tasks:

1. Elect a chairperson for your delegation.
2. Inventory your nation's food supply and compare it to your needs.
3. Examine the position statements below and decide what course of action your country should take.
4. Your chairperson should be prepared to present a 5 minute statement of position at the meeting of the General Assembly and all members of the delegation should be ready to defend your nation's position.

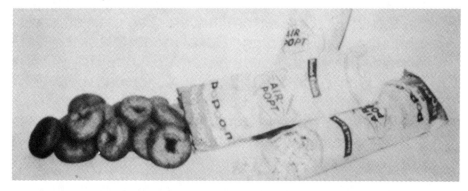

POSITION STATEMENTS (GREAT DONUT CRISIS)

A. THE UNITED STATES OF DONUTS
   You have plenty of food to feed your population and enough left over to export to other countries. Your problem is that your people do not want to give away your food to the needy. The

donut makers want higher prices and everyone in your country is satisfied because they have all of the donuts that they can eat at prices they can afford. WHAT IS YOUR NATION'S POSITION?

B. THE REPUBLIC OF BAD NEWS

Your country has a population problem and on top of that most of your land area is not suited for agriculture. Furthermore, both your people and your government are very poor and cannot afford modern donut making equipment that is needed to feed your people. At the conference, you must look to the other two nations for help. What does your nation have to offer in the bargaining? WHAT IS YOUR NATION'S POSITION?

C. THE FEDERATION OF BIG BUSINESS

Your country cannot produce enough food but you have plenty of industry and money to import all that you need from the U.S. of Donuts. However, your economy depends on the sea route and ports of Bad News and you have been good allies with the Bad News Republic for over 100 years. You have called this conference in your capital city to try to help in this crisis. WHAT IS YOUR NATION'S POSITION AND HOW WILL YOU PERSUADE THE UNITED STATES OF DONUTS TO HELP YOUR FRIENDS IN BAD NEWS?

POSITION STATEMENTS (GREAT POPCORN CRISIS)

A. THE PEOPLE'S REPUBLIC OF POPCORN

You are a very rich agricultural nation which produces 90% of your continent's main foodstuff, popcorn. Of this popcorn crop, your country needs only 50% to feed itself, so that 50% is shipped out of the country. Most of those exports goes to the United States of Hot Air, which supplies your country with most of its energy in the form of hot air. The present crisis developed when the Kingdom of the Do-Without's blockaded the Long and Winding River, thus cutting off the main trade route between your country and the U.S. of H.A. Your assignment is to obtain the desperately needed trade route through the Kingdom of the Do-Withouts. Keep in mind that your nation is in need of more hot air and faces the chance of spoilage of this year's huge popcorn crop.

B. THE KINGDOM OF THE DO-WITHOUT'S

Your country is very poor and produces only 5% of the popcorn supply. This small amount will just barely supply the needs of 50% of your population. In the past, most of your government's money has gone to buy food to feed the starving people of your country. The popcorn is bought from the P.R.P. at very high prices. However, there is now talk of spending that money on guns and patrol boats in order to completely control the long and Winding River to force P.R.P. to lower its prices. The blockade had already begun. It is up to you to try to get more popcorn for your country. It should be noted, however, that every day of the military blockade is costing your country millions of dollars and causes more people to face the threat of starvation. You must decide how to act in the best interest of your people.

C. THE UNITED STATES OF HOT AIR
Your country is very small and mountainous and produces only 5% of the popcorn supply. This will feed only 50% of your population. However, your country has a supply of hot air, which is desperately needed by the People's Republic of Popcorn to run its popcorn factories. Now that the Kingdom of the Do-Without's has begun its blockade, you have a large supply of hot air but are running low on food to feed your hot air factory workers. Find a solution for your country's problem.

(Contributed by Ed Tarvin, Bentonville, Arkansas)

GUEST SPEAKER FROM THE EARLY DAYS

This role play is an effective way to help youth explore the personalities and feelings of Biblical characters who often seem unreal. Combined with a Bible study, it can add a great deal of depth to the learning experience.

A Biblical character is selected and someone in the group (perhaps the youth director) first researches that character and then assumes the identity of that character in a speech to the entire group. For example, he could "become" Peter, and try to relate to the group his reactions and feelings when:

1. Andrew first introduced him to Jesus.
2. Jesus stepped into his boat and addressed the crowd.
3. Peter walked on the water.
4. Peter confessed Christ as Lord and then immediately rebuked Him for speaking of His death.
5. Peter refused (at first) to have his feet washed by Jesus.
6. The events of Maundy Thursday unfolded.
7. Peter denied Christ.
8. Christ spoke to Peter on the beach after His resurrection.

Following the speech, the group can question "Peter" about the things he said, and "Peter" can respond as he feels the real Peter would have. For further discussion the group can then be divided into smaller groups and discuss related questions such as:

1. If you were one of the other disciples, how would you feel about Christ spending so much time with Peter?

2. If someone did to you what Peter did to Christ, how would you feel?
3. What do the words of Christ to Peter on the beach after His resurrection tell you about Christ's love for Peter?
4. When have you ever felt like Peter in any of these situations?

This same approach can be used with any of a number of personalities from the Bible. It is guaranteed to get your group thinking in new ways about the pioneers of our faith. (Contributed by Arlin Migliazzo, Ellensburg, Washington)

HERE COMES THE BRIDE

Invite several couples to come speak to your senior high group about the difference between a wedding and being married. Invite the kids to come to the meeting with wedding announcements, have a big wedding cake, photographer, reception, and the whole bit. Ask the ladies to bring their wedding gowns (if they still have them) and to model them (if they can still get into them). Have the pastor go through the wedding ceremony, explaining the various parts of it, why they are included, etc. After the reception (or whenever) have a discussion. The couples selected to participate should have different years experience: one year, five years, fifteen years, twenty-five years or more. Begin by having them describe their wedding day and talk briefly about how their lives and their relationship has changed (or not changed) over the years. Then allow the kids to ask questions. You'll be amazed at how many they will have. (Contributed by Pastor David, Silver Spring, Maryland)

HOW GOD SEES ME

Each person is asked to take a sheet of newsprint and on one side draw pictures, cartoons, or sayings expressing "How I See God." The other side is to be filled with symbols expressing "How I Think God Sees Me." Allow 20-25 minutes to complete. After everyone is finished, each person should explain their drawing to the entire group. This exercise opens a group up to sharing where each one stands with God at present and demonstrates the varying facets of an individual's experience with God. (Contributed by David Markle, Hickory, North Carolina)

HUMAN CONTINUUM

When discussing subjects that have many points of view, have the kids arrange themselves (prior to the discussion) on a "Human continuum" from one extreme viewpoint to the opposite extreme. For example, if you are discussing "drinking", have the kids line up with all those who are "for" drinking on one end, and those who are "against" it at the other. Undecideds or moderates would be somewhere in the middle.

FOR   AGAINST
├──┤

Kids may discuss the issue among themselves as they attempt to find the right spot in the line in relationship to each other. After they are settled, further discussion or debate can take place as kids attempt to defend their positions. Anyone may change positions at anytime. (Contributed by Mike Renquist, Dallas, Texas)

IMAGE OF CHRIST

Here's a short discussion starter on the person of Jesus Christ. Divide the group into small groups and give each group one of the Scripture references given below to discuss. Then have each group come up with the scriptural "image of Christ" that was in their selection. Have one person in each group give the class the image discovered in their findings.

Scripture:
1. Phillipians 2:5-11
2. Matthew 25:34-40
3. Isaish 42:1-9
4. John 10:11-16
5. John 6:44-51
6. Luke 4:38-44
7. Matthew 16:13-

Image:
1. Lord and Servant
2. Kind and Friend
3. Suffering Servant
4. Shepherd
5. Teacher and bringer of life
6. Compassionate
7. Peter's confession

(Contributed by Sr. Eleanor Hoffmann, Peoria, Illinois)

INVENT

Divide your youth group into smaller groups of 8 to 10. Describe the situation below and give each group twenty minutes to finish their task. At the end of the allotted time, have the group all meet together and compare their responses.

Situation: You find yourself in a new civilization in which everything is the same as our world is now, but there is no Bible, no God, no religion, no church, no religious history. You have been selected by your government to create a God that will have the proper attributes that will cause people to worship. This God should represent everything that you think will be attractive and yet as the same time, explain things like natural disasters (flood, earthquake, etc.), sickness, suffering, and evil.

Questions to help you as you invent God: What is its name, if any? Where does it live? Is it visible? Will your God make any demands on people? How do you worship it? Any rewards or punishments? What does it look like? Is there more than one? Does it have any bad attributes? Just let your imaginations run wild and attempt to invent the "perfect" God that will attract the most people.

The discussion should then compare the invented God with the God of the Bible. The following questions could be included in the discussion:

1. Why is God so mysterious?
2. Why did God leave so many unanswered questions?
3. Why doesn't God make Himself visible?
4. What are the most difficult things about God to believe?
5. What things would you change about God if you could?

(Adapted from an idea contributed by Timothy Quill, Appleton, Wisconsin)

LIFE AUCTION

Divide your group into small groups and give each group a sheet like the one below. After each group finishes their sheet, bidding begins. After the auction is over, the whole group then discusses and evaluates what happened. The items below could be changed and adapted to fit your particular group.

LIFE AUCTION

You have received $5,000.00 and can spend the money any way you desire. Budget the money in the column labeled "AMOUNT BUDGETED". We will then bid on each item in an Auction manner. It is YOUR GOAL to gain the things you most desire.

	AMOUNT Budgeted	AMOUNT SPENT	HIGHEST BID	
1. A wonderful family life without any hassles.				
2. All the money I need to be happy.				
3. Never to be sick.				
4. To find the right mate, who is good-looking and fulfills me.				
5. Never to have pimples.				
6. To be able to do whatever I want whenever I want.				
7. To have all the power the President has.				
8. To be the best looking person.				
9. To have a real hunger to always read the Bible.				
10. To be able to understand all things.				
11. To eliminate all hunger and disease in the world.				
12. To always be close to God.				
13. Never to feel lonely or put down.				
14. Always be happy and peaceful.				
15. Never feel hurt.				
16. To own a beautiful home, car, boat, plane and 7 motorcycles for each day of the week.				
17. To be super smart without ever having to attend school.				
18. To be able to excel fast and superior in all things.				
19. To be filled with God's presence in the most dynamic way.				

20. To always know that you are in God's Will.				
21. To be the greatest athlete in the world.				
22. To be looked up to by everyone else.				
23. To become a star on "Welcome Back Kotter".				
24. To always have a lot of close friends who never let you down.				
25. To walk close to God.				

LIVING CHRISTMAS GIFT

Here is a clever and meaningful Christmas gift suggestion that will become more valuable as the years go by. Have your young people interview their grandparents about their experiences in life. (Sort of an autobiography on tape.) Suggest that the young people duplicate the tape and give a copy to each of the relatives for Christmas.

LONG DISTANCE ROLE PLAY

Here's an interesting role play using simulated telephone conversations. Give each person a card with one of the following situations written on it. They must act out only one side of the conversation, and the rest of the group then tries to guess what is going on.

1. You have just called heaven to complain about the way things are going and after you have listed all your complaints you find you were talking to God personally.
2. God has just called you to suggest that you break up with your boyfriend/girlfriend and you are trying to convince Him otherwise.
3. God has just called to explain that He wants you to be a missionary. You don't so you're trying to convince Him that you do, but not right now.
4. God called and wants you to give an account of how you have spent the last three days.
5. You have just experienced a personal tragedy and you call God to ask why? He answers the phone, listens to what you have to say and then hangs up without a word.

(Contributed by Marja L. Coons, Albuquerque, New Mexico)

LOOK AT THE BOOK

Here is a great discussion starter. The true/false statements below can be very effective in helping your young people determine their attitudes about the Bible and in helping you discover what your group thinks of the Bible.

Duplicate the following list of statements and have each member of your group take the test by writing "true" or "false" after each one. Then go back and discuss each question in detail.

1. The Bible is a record of man's search for God.
2. The Bible is like a scientific textbook when it describes the origin of the world.
3. The Bible is primarily a factual history of the Jewish people.
4. The Bible contains detailed answers to all of man's questions.
5. The Bible needs to be interpreted literally.
6. The main thrust of the Biblical witness is the description of ethical norms. (What is right and what is wrong.)
7. Every part of the Bible has the same level of importance as every other part.
8. One needs to read the Bible as a spectator rather than as a participant.
9. The Bible was written and compiled all at once.
10. All the writings in the Bible are a response to God's activity and concern for His people.
11. The Bible can prove the existence of God.
12. A person's job in studying the Bible is to learn to ask the right questions.
13. The Bible is a recital of history without interruption.
14. There is no other truth about God than what is disclosed in the Bible.
15. The Old Testament has no relevance for today.
16. The Bible is basically one story...that of God's search for communion with man.

(Contributed by Jim Kirkpatrick, Newton, North Carolina)

THE LOST COIN

Hide a silver dollar (or half dollar) somewhere in the room and announce that whoever finds it can keep it. After the coin is found, gather the group together and discuss the parable of the "lost coin" found in Luke 15. Ask the one who found the coin what he or she plans to do with it. From this a parallel can be drawn between how the coin is to be used and how God wants to use us, rather than simply putting us on the shelf. This simulation/illustration is best with junior high and younger. (Contributed by Rich Young, Hanford, California)

LOVE IS A HUG

This idea is very similar to "Groupers" found in *Ideas Number Two*. But rather than writing a word response to a phrase like "love is...", you have the kids draw a cartoon representing what love is. This can be used with all the "fruits of the Spirit" and many other subjects. Do this periodically and display the cartoons in the youth room. (Contributed by Melissa Reynolds, Hanford, California)

LOVE LISTS

Spend some time as a group reading and relating to various scripture texts that deal with the subject of love. Possible choices might be the Cain and Abel story (Genesis 4), the words of Jesus concerning "the least of these" (Matthew 25), or numerous other passages that deal with relationships between people.

Then divide into small groups and supply each person with pencil and paper. Each person should make four columns on the paper with the following headings: 1. "Intimate" 2. "Close" 3. "Acquaintances" 4. "Distant." Under each column, names of people are listed according to how "intimate" or "distant" they might be. Maximum for any column should be five (or so) names. The names can be friends and acquaintances at church, school, work, family, or elsewhere.

After each person has listed names under each column, have a time for sharing in the small groups. Each person should explain why certain people were listed under the various column headings and whether or not they are satisfied with their lists as they stand. Here they may share feelings, experiences, school or living situations that contributed to the list choices. In addition, have each person examine their lists again and pick out one name from the "acquaintances" or "distant" columns, and think specifically about ways to become closer to that person so that they might move up one column. Close with a chance for people in the group to share feelings of closeness or distance that they feel with other members of the group. (Contributed by Jim Thompson, Littleton, Colorado)

LUTTS AND MIPPS

Pretend that *lutts and mipps* represent a new way of measuring distance, and that *dars, wors, and mirs* represent a new way of measuring time. A man drives from Town "A" through Town "B" and Town "C" to Town "D." The task of your group is to determine how many *wors* the entire trip took. You have twenty minutes for this task. Do not choose a formal leader. You will be given bits of information that relates to the task of your group. You may share the information orally, but you must keep the written information in your hands throughout.

Divide into small groups fo four or five and distribute the above instructions to each group. Then pass out one, two, or three cards to each person (they don't have to have the same number of cards, just shuffle and pass out all eight). The cards contain the information:

Card 1: Town A is 16 lutts from Town C
Card 2: Town B is 10 lutts, 6 mipps from Town D
Card 3: Town C is halfway between Town B and Town D
Card 4: The man is riding in a horse and buggy
Card 5: The man's average speed is 1 lutt per dar
Card 6: 10 wors equal 1 dar
Card 7: 10 mipps equal 1 lutt
Card 8: 10 mirs equal 1 wor

This, by the way, is a problem from a fourth grade math book. The problem solving experience shows us several things:

1. *Group dynamics:* Who was the leader? Why did you react the way you did? Did you feel a part of your group or like an outsider? Was there a sense of competition? Why or why not? How did you feel when the other group(s) finished before you? Etc...

2. *Individual worth:* You have to sort out the information, which means you have to get all of it first. When working with youth, it is important to get all the information about them you can. This comes by being their friend and they begin to open up to you. You must use the right information and disregard the meaningless. (Have you ever noticed in board meetings that some guy always seems to think "But he's riding a horse and buggy" is the most important information?)

3. *Definition of terms:* We know the "lingo," but do we really know what it means? We toss around church words a lot, but do we take the time to ask ourselves and our youth, "What does that really mean?" Do we go through the motions without realizing what it means? And what about visitors to the group? Do we assume that they will know what "justification" or "communion" or even who Jesus Christ is so that they leave confused because we didn't take the time to explain it to them? We need to discipline ourselves to talk the language that the people we try to communicate with can understand. And first, we need to clarify that meaning in our own life.

(Contributed by Larry Jansen, Indianapolis, Indiana)

THE MAN FROM ICK

The following parable has many discussion possibilities. Simply read it to the group and provide time to discuss its meaning. Some sample questions are provided, although many others are also possible.

Once there was a town called Ick.
The people of Ick had a problem. They were icky.
For some unexplained reason, everyone who was born in Ick ended up icky. Scientists, doctors, experts from all over the world had tried to

analyze the people of Ick, and although they all agreed that the people of Ick were icky, no one could agree on a cure. In fact, there was no cure.

The scientists, doctors and experts agreed that the only thing they could do would be to give people suggestions on how to cope with their ickyness.

But experts or no experts, everyone learned to cope in their own way. Some pretended they weren't icky. Some tried to keep busy and forget their ickyness. Others decided that being icky was better than not being icky...and they got ickier.

Some just didn't care.

Usually, if you were able to get a person from Ick to be honest, they really didn't like being icky.

Well, you can imagine how many people arrived in Ick with a "cure" for ickyness. And you can imagine how many people were always willing to try each new "cure" that came along. And strangely enough, some of the "cures" seemed to work... for a while. But eventually, the cure would stop working and everyone would be icky again.

One day something happened that would radically change the people of Ick.

A long-time resident of Ick began to suggest publicly that he had a cure for ickyness.

It was very difficult for the people of Ick to believe that a person who lived in Ick himself could have a real cure for ickyness.

But then something strange happened. One of the ickiest people in all of Ick believed in this cure and was changed. He simply wasn't icky anymore. Everyone thought it was just temporary and waited. But it didn't go away and before long, lots and lots of people started believing the man from Ick...and everyone who believed was cured.

It was incredible and one would think that the people of Ick were overjoyed.

But the people weren't overjoyed and soon a town meeting was called. The fact of the matter was, the business community of Ick had been built around the basic fact of people's ickyness.

And with more and more people losing their ickyness, the economic future of Ick was threatened. After an extremely heated discussion, it was generally agreed that what appeared to be a cure for ickyness was probably like all the other so-called cures and would soon turn out to be a hoax. And since so many people were being misled and since it was possible that many more people could be misled, and since a person who would perpetuate such a hoax on a community like Ick could affect the "stability" of Ick, the "saviour" of Ick was asked to leave.

He refused.

He continued to cure people and each day those responsible for the "stability" of Ick became more and more concerned. One day the "saviour" of Ick disappeared. It caused quite a commotion and no one to this day knows what happened. Some say he had been done away with. Others said they had actually seen him the day after he disappeared. But what was strange was that even though the "saviour" of Ick was gone, people who believed in him and his cure would suddenly find their ickyness gone. And even though the majority of the townspeople were in agreement that this "saviour" was, in fact a hoax, all those who had believed in him were still cured.

The people who had lost their ickyness thought everyone would jump at the chance to be cured. They were sadly disappointed. Very few were even interested. So the ex-icky people did what they could to convince the icky people that their cure was not a hoax and every once in a while someone would believe.

Apparently, and this is only hearsay, a small group of ex-icky people began to worry that if they or their children associated too much with icky people, they might be contaminated or become icky again.

It wasn't long before these people banded together and moved to the top of Ick Hill, an isolated spot on the edge of town. They would work, shop,

109

and go to school in downtown Ick and then return to Ick Hill for their evenings and weekends. But it wasn't long before the people of Ick Hill became so fearful of contamination that they built their own school, market, gas station, and shopping center.

A few more months went by.

And one morning the people of Ick woke up to see Ick Hill covered by a large glass bubble. Ick Hill was now a completely self-contained community with everything completely under control.

One particularly cold morning, an icky person in the city of Ick noticed that there was no visible activity going on inside the glass bubble of Ick Hill. A rescue party was sent to see if everything was alright.

After breaking through the glass bubble, they were shocked to find the entire population of Ick Hill dead. Autopsies were ordered and the cause of death was the same for all.

Suffocation.

Questions for discussion:

1. Is it a legitimate function of the church to "protect" its people?
2. What things in the church "suffocate" you. What things in the church are like fresh air.
3. What do you think of church schools, Christian "Yellow Pages", Christian communes?
4. What does it mean to be "in the world, but not of it"?
5. Can you separate from the world without being isolated from the world?

(Adapted from an idea contributed by Joe Falkner, Fort Worth, Texas)

MEDITATING DAY AND NIGHT

Starting off with the mind-blowing idea that people actually loved to meditate on the Old Testament law "day and night" (see Psalm 1:2 and Psalm 119 in its mammoth entirety), have your kids pick two of the Ten Commandments (each individual makes a personal choice), isolate themselves and meditate on them for five to ten minutes. Tell them that nothing much happens in meditation for the first five minutes, so be patient. After they've had some time to get quiet, introduce a couple of questions for them to think about:

1. What kind of world would it be if everyone obeyed this commandment?
2. What kind of world would it be if nobody obeyed it?

Following the meditation period, have the kids share some of their thoughts relating to the specific commandments they chose. The following discussion questions can be used:

1. Which commandments did you choose and why?
2. How would you answer the previous two questions (What kind of world....)?
3. Why do you think Biblical commands are resisted so much

today?

4. Do Christians still have to obey Old Testament laws?
5. Are laws necessary in the church?
6. Which laws are hard for you to obey?

(Contributed by Dave Phillips, Old Greenwich, Connecticut)

NAME THAT JESUS

Many of us have our conception of Jesus Christ influenced heavily by pictures we have seen of Christ. Ask your young people to write down a description of what they think Christ looked like. Follow that with a comparison of each person's description and a discussion of the physical appearance of Jesus.

Then bring before the group as many different pictures of Jesus as you can find. Discuss each picture and attempt to write a description of the group's response to the picture. (For example, Hook's famous picture of Christ could be described by "strong, masculine, compassionate, determined, intense, healthy, handsome, etc.") You could also discuss different movies or plays where Christ was portrayed and compare each of those.

© 1967 ALL RIGHTS RESERVED.
R. COBB

As a finale to this lengthy discussion, take different Scriptural passages dealing with Jesus and attempt to formulate, as a group, what you think Jesus looked like and why. (Don't be limited to New Testament references to Christ. Include Isaiah 53:1-3 and Psalms 22:6-8.) (Contributed by Michael McDowell, Rilliant, Ohio)

NEW YEAR'S RESOLUTIONS

First discuss the meaning of the words "New Year's Resolution." Ask kids to share some that they have made in the past and what happened to them. Did they last? How long? Next, introduce the word "covenant," and ask kids to compare that word with the word "resolution." What is the difference between the two? (One important difference is that a resolution is generally a private thing, and a covenant is a promise or agreement made publicly between two or more people.)

After some discussion, have the kids form small groups of three, preferably with friends that they know fairly well. Then give them ten minutes or so to write a few "New Year's Covenants." After they are completed, each person then shares his or her covenants with other members of the small group and asks for feedback. Are they too vague? Impossible to keep? Too easy? Inappropriate? Each person then is allowed to rewrite his or her covenants based on the feedback received. Finally, the kids share their rewritten covenants and perhaps discuss practical ways they plan to put them into practice. (Contributed by J. Richard Short, Metairie, Louisiana)

OBSERVERS

Before your youth meeting begins, choose three kids to serve as observers. (Often times it is best to do this privately so nobody in the group is aware of it.) In choosing your observers, special thought should be taken as to who you pick, and why. You may want to enlist someone who usually does not get involved, or someone who is especially optimistic, or maybe someone who is able to give constructive criticism.

Throughout the entire evening, they are to sit back and observe what is really taking place. They should watch for things like:

1. How does the group work together?
2. Who are the leaders?
3. Were there any good ideas expressed by people that were missed, ignored or overlooked?
4. Is the group positive or negative, exciting or blaah?
5. Do the people in the group *really* care about each other? How?
6. If a visitor were to walk into the room, what would he think? Why?

At the end of the meeting, have the observers report their observations. Then discuss what positive changes can be made. (Contributed by Timothy Quill, Appleton, Wisconsin)

OBSTACLE ILLUSION

Here is an activity that is not only fun but has great discussion potential. It is a combination trust walk and obstacle course. First of all, you will need a large area with a lot of minor obstacles such as light poles, trees, playground equipment, etc. (one group used the church boiler room after they had shut down all of the heating and cooling equipment.) Then pick a starting point and run some heavy cord to the nearest obstacle. At that point string out two or more lines to other nearby obstacles. Only one line will continue beyond one of the obstacles, the others will dead end. Continue the main line to the next obstacle with more dead ends, etc. Mark the end of the line by hanging a coffee can full of marbles from the last obstacle. Divide into small groups of 8-12 kids. Have each group choose a leader and two or three assistants. Line the kids up in a hand-on-shoulder single file line and blindfold each one (unless you are in a room and can make it absolutely dark). Lead each group separately by a confusing path to the starting point and let each group follow the course alone.

Explain to the groups that the object is to follow the main line together without separating. (The leader can stop the group while he/she sends out assistants to check when they come to more than one line.)

Note: Be sure to vary the heights of the line. For example, if the main line leads to an obstacle at shoulder level, it could go out from the obstacle at knee or ankle level while a dead end continues from shoulder level. Also plan obstacles that require the kids to stoop under. Make sure the course is long enough so that it takes 20 to 25 minutes to finish! (Contributed by Bob Kerstetter, Plano, Texas)

OLD TESTAMENT TIME MACHINE

Here's a creative way to get your junior high group interested in the Old Testament. Build a "Time Machine" with all kinds of creative lights and sounds. When the button is pushed, it makes all kinds of weird noises and then begins to speak. As it speaks it can produce some sheets of paper with the questions reprinted along with space to answer them.

Time Machine:

Just can't keep your finger off that button can you? The year is 870 B.C. Your view finder comes upon "Elijah", the great warrior prophet for God. You've heard a lot of good things about Elijah, yet now you see him sulking and complaining that he's no good, that he's a complete failure.

Printed Sheets:

Remember how Elijah challenged the prophets of Baal by showing that God would bring fire and burn up the offerings? Well, that wasn't such a good idea 'cause now everybody's real upright with Elijah. But—HOW WOULD YOU HAVE DONE IT? What kind of contest would you have had to determine who the real God was? Describe it on the back: Then meet together in groups of three and share your ideas. Come up with an award winning idea and then the whole class can judge it and send it in to your favorite newsletter.

Time Machine:

O.K. Back to the view finder . . . Elijah is really upset. I mean he feels like the *pits.* Elijah feels that way because a lot of people are really down on him.

Printed Sheets:

Of the following people, who gets down on you the most?
_____parents
_____friends
_____teachers
_____brothers
_____sisters

If you had to be harassed by some people, which of the following would you really not want to be harassed by?
_____the police
_____the Mafia
_____the Hell's Angels
_____the C.I.A.
_____the Pittsburgh Steelers

Time Machine:

Hey, the voice scanner just picked up a conversation between God and Elijah. It seems that God found Elijah hiding in a cave. What do you think each of them said to the other?

Printed Sheets:

Describe the conversation between God and Elijah:
Elijah:
God:
Elijah:
God:
Elijah:
God:

Time Machine:

Well, Elijah finally gets the word to get back to work and stop pouting and sulking. What about you? What's something you've been kind of sulking about lately? Write it down and then get together with one other person and share it. (Allow time for this.)

Time Machine:

Whoops! A malfunction and you can't quite get back into the 20th century. So you end up about 783 B.C. Who's the man stomping angrily in circles, shaking his fist towards Heaven? Why it's Jonah! Told to go and preach repentance to Ninevah, a city in Assyria and Assyria was one of Israel's worst enemies. So Jonah didn't want God to forgive such a wicked enemy.

Printed Sheets:

What country would be to the U.S. like Assyria was to Israel? Does God love the people of that country as much as He loves us?

Time Machine:

Well, there goes Jonah on the big banana boat and he's not going to Ninevah and preach about no repentance. He's headed for Tarshish, the fun city. Is he scared, bored, angry, nervous or what? Wait! There's a letter on the pier that Jonah left addressed to God.

Printed Sheets:

What do you think the letter to God from Jonah says?
  Dear God,

                              Very truly yours,
                              Jonah

Time Machine:

What about you? Ever feel like God was after you? Or maybe your folks, or the church or your friends? What do you do to escape? And if you don't escape, then what do you do to just plain relax sometimes and get away from it all? Jot down a few ideas that you could share in the group of 2 or 3 people and then report back to the larger group. (Allow time for this.)

Printed sheets:

On the scales below, write a number between 1 and 10 that described how much you obey God in the following things:

1. Prayer life	1 2 3 4 5 6 7 8 9 10
2. Witnessing about your faith	1 2 3 4 5 6 7 8 9 10
3. Honoring your parents	1 2 3 4 5 6 7 8 9 10
4. Loving your enemies	1 2 3 4 5 6 7 8 9 10
5. Reading the Bible	1 2 3 4 5 6 7 8 9 10
6. Helping others less fortunate than you	1 2 3 4 5 6 7 8 9 10

(Contributed by George Gaffga, Liberty Corner, New Jersey)

ONE-POT POT-LUCK SOUP-SUPPER

Here's an idea that's a variation on the old friendship salad. It's a great way to dramatize several issues, like world hunger and how our small individual efforts can make the difference when added to the whole, and more generally, the meaning of the Body of Christ as the union of all of the gifts and individual contributions of its members.

Before the meeting, have someone boil several soup bones, add salt and herbs to make a hearty broth. This can be made well in advance and frozen, but must be thawed completely and for best results, boiling rapidly at the very beginning of the meeting. Each person brings his favorite vegetable like a carrot or celery stick, onion, tomato, etc., or some grain or legume like rice or noodles, beans or barley. Each of these in whatever small quantities they arrive are added to the broth. Make sure you add the beans and grains first, followed by the vegetables. The whole thing should need about one or one and a half hours to cook at a good pace. While the soup is cooking, have a film or speaker with the focus on world hunger, or some crowd breakers or community building exercises to dramatize further the nature of the Body of Christ.

After an hour or so, serve the soup and see how amazed everyone is that their tiny offering of a vegetable fit together so well with everyone else's to make a hearty and good tasting soup. (Contributed by James Ward, Saratoga, California)

PARABLE OF THE SHAPES

The following play is excellent for use in conjunction with a discussion or meeting with a "love" theme. It is based on the idea that there are basically three kinds of love: "if" love, "because" love, and "in-spite-of" love (which is the best kind, of course).

The characters each carry a large cardboard shape as their costume. Their identities thus become their shapes. The "Blob" should carry a crumpled-up newspaper or some other nondescript shape, and the "In-spite-of" Man carries no shape at all.

The Script:

Narrator:
There once was a land of If and Because
That sat on the earth as every land does.
And every person who lived in the land
Would search for a person he could understand
Now let us together observe what takes place
When If and Because people meet face-to-face . . .

1st Circle:
As I walk along this fine sunny day,
A stranger I see coming my way.
Is he a friend or is he a foe?
Not til I look at his shape will I know.
A circle I be and a circle I stay.
A circle is needed for friendship today.
(Enter the Blob.)
Hello my friend, Circle's my name
And finding a friend is my kind of game.
Have you a circle to exchange with me here?
Or are you an alien shape, I fear?

Blob:
A friendly fellow you seem to be
And circles I need for good friends to be.
What my own shape is, I really don't know
But I hope its a circle so friendship will grow.
I'm so glad I found you, I'm so glad to see
That such a relationship can possibly be.

1st Circle:
Now wait a minute, oh stranger here.
You hasten your happiness too fast I fear.
I told you before our two shapes must match
In order for any new friendship to hatch.
If you were a circle with roundest of frame,
We'd be friends forever because we're the same.
But I see no circle, I see nothing round.
I think that it's only a Blob that I've found.
Now think of my image, what others might say,
I can't take the risk. Away! Away!

Blob: I'm so broken hearted, I'm in such despair.
I am not a circle. It doesn't seem fair.
(Enter 2nd Circle.)

2nd Circle: A call for a circle, is that what I hear?
I too am a circle, such joy and such cheer!
For now, brother Circle, your long vigil ends.
We've found one another. Forever we're friends!
(Two circles embrace and walk off.)

1st Star: I am a star, a beautiful star.
Better than all other shapes, by far.
And if you are the finest, I think you will see
That shape you are holding, a star it will be.
If I'd find a star, we'd frolic in fun
And dance and play and never be done.
If you are a star, my friendship you've won.
But as I look closer, I see you're not one.
You're only a Blob! We'll never go far,
Unless you can prove that you're also a star!

Blob: My shape's not important. Myself is what counts.
Just give me some friendship in any amount.

1st Star: I've no time for Blobs, so go on your way,
For I think a star is coming this way . . .
(Enter 2nd star.)

2nd Star: A star I am, and a star I'll stay.
Oh praise be to stars, it's our lucky day!

1st Star: O star, o star, what double delight!
These shapes that we're holding, they match us just right.

2nd Star: At last we're together, so happy and proud.
Together we'll surely stand out in a crowd.
So Blob, adios! Farewell and goodbye!
You just don't fit in, and don't ask us why.

Blob: Alas, I am broken. What worse could I do?
Than being rejected by each of these two.
(Enter 1st square.)

1st Square: Through this crowd I now will stare
To see if perhaps there be somewhere a square.
Pardon me there, but some time could you lend?
If you are a square, I'll be your true friend.

118

Blob:	Oh surely, dear brother, our shape's not the same, But I'm a sweet person, and what's in a name?
1st Square:	Your shape's not a square and you talk to me so? I can't believe all the nerve that you show. If it's friendship you want, then friendship go get. But not from a shape with which you don't fit! *(Enter 2nd square.)*
2nd Square:	A call for a square? I'll soon be right there! A square I am and a square I'll be. I'll join you in friendship, oh square, just ask me. Because our fine corners do each number four, We'll stay close together forever and more! *(They both exit.)*
Blob:	I'm torn and I'm frazzled, what worse could there be, Than being rejected by each of these three. *(Enter 1st Triangle.)*
1st Triangle:	I'm wandering to and I'm wandering fro, In search of a three-sided shape just like so. *(points)* For if I could find one, I know we would blend, For only a triangle can be a true friend.
Blob:	Hello there, dear fellow, I've heard all you've said, I can't help but thinking, to you I've been led. For you need friendship and I need the same. So on with the friendship and off with the game.
1st Triangle:	Now who is this talking? What shape do you hold? You seem sort of strange, just what is your mold? You sure are not pretty, you shapeless disgrace. Why, you're just a Blob, it's all over your face! I've no time for you, you pitiful one. This senseless discussion is over and done! *(Enter 2nd Triangle.)*
2nd Triangle:	A call for triangles? Well I'll fill the need. We're made for each other, it must be agreed! *(They exit together.)*
Blob:	No one understands poor shapeless me, Cause I'm just a Blob as you can well see. If I were a circle or maybe a square, Then I could be having some fun over there. Why can't all you shapes just notice and see, That I'm just as miserable as I can be. With no one to laugh and be good friends with, I'm beginning to feel just a little bit miffed.
Narrator:	Now just at this moment comes into this place A man who is different in style and in grace. He's quiet and thoughtful and listens quite well, Observing the stories that our characters tell. Now with me return to our tale if you can, And witness the ways of "In-Spite-Of" Man. *(Enter In-Spite-Of Man.)*
In-Spite-Of Man:	Hello, will you be my friend?
Blob:	Oh, no, can't you see . . . I'm not a circle or square, so please leave me be.
In-Spite-Of Man:	Friend, once again to you I will say, Will you not be my friend on this fine day?
Blob:	Your humor's not funny. I'm wise to your jokes. You're here to make fun like the rest of these folks.
In-Spite-Of Man:	Now what is the problem, my poor little man? You seem so distressed, I just can't understand.

119

Blob:

I've run the whole gamit, I've pleaded and cried
To have them accept me and love me inside.
But each time I seek them they look at my shape,
And quickly reject me, it's like hearing a tape.
"You're not the right person, you've got the wrong shape,
The people will gossip, the people will gape."
If this shall continue from day unto day,
Alone I'll remain and depressed will I stay.

In-Spite-Of Man:

I think a great lesson's been brought to your sight.
These shapes find it hard to accept you "in spite".
They're all so possessive and selfish inside,
They wallow in vanity, ego, and pride.
But there is an answer I've found to be true,
And I've come to offer this answer to you.

Blob:

I don't understand all you're trying to say,
But you're the first person I've met here today
Who seems to accept me in spite of my form
You break all the rules of the shape-seekers norm.

In-Spite-Of Man:

Your wisdom is growing, I think you now see
Love puts no conditions on you or on me.

Narrator:

Our moral is simple, I'll share it with you.
It's all in the Bible and known to be true.
The world offers values which dazzle our eyes,
It mixes the truth with ridiculous lies.
And we here are seeking the true meaning of
This life that we're living. This word we call "love".
The If and Because folks are caught in a bind,
For they only accept their very own kind.
They love folks "because" and they love people "if",
But few have discovered the "In-Spite-Of" Gift!

(Contributed by Dick Davis, Minneapolis, Minnesota)

PARAPHRASING THE LOVE CHAPTER

Here is a way to allow kids the opportunity to put some of their own thoughts into the "Love Chapter" of the Bible, I Corinthians 13. By doing an exercise such as this (it can be done with other portions of Scripture as well), it forces kids to think through the meaning and application of the passage. Leave key words or phrases out of the verse, but leave enough in that the basic idea will still be communicated. Have the kids then fill in the blanks with whatever they think fits best for them. Afterwards, compare with the message of the original. The following is an example. Just print it up and pass it out. Let each person read their completed version to the entire group.

I Corinthians 13

If I have all the ability to talk about _____, but have no love, then I am nothing but a big mouth. If I had all the power to _____, but have no love, then my life is a waste of time. If I understand everything about _____, but have no love, then I might as well sit in a gutter. If I give away everything that I have, but have no love, then I _____. Love is patient, love is kind, love is _____. Love never _____

(Contributed by George Gaffga, Liberty Corner, New Jersey)

PARENT PANEL

This is an excellent transgenerational exercise that can give your youth group an opportunity to understand the parent's point of view. Although this particular idea deals with the subject of dating, any subject could be used by following the guidelines given below.

Choose two moms and two dads to be the panelists. (CAUTION: Do not choose panelists who are related to anyone in your youth group. Do not choose a husband and wife on the same panel. And be sure the panelists have been parents of teenagers who have already passed the dating stage.)

About two weeks before the scheduled panel discussion, have your youth group submit, anonymously, their questions about dating. After all the questions have been submitted, go through and eliminate duplicates, reword poorly stated questions, and then prepare a master list of questions. Duplicate the list and give each panelist a copy a week in advance. On the night of the panel, give each of the young people a copy so they can follow along and take notes.

The leader moderates the meeting, going through question by question, before opening the discussion to the group at large. (Contributed by Tom Bougher, Little Rock, Arkansas)

PAUL'S LETTER TO THE AMERICANS

This is an activity that causes both the kids and leader to reflect on their present lives and help them get a feeling for Paul's letters to the churches.

Have the kids write a letter to themselves from "Paul" praising (it's important to praise as well as admonish) and admonishing themselves on their lifestyle. Give them about twenty minutes then break into small groups and have them share their letters.

Another adaptation is to use a specific passage (Ephesians 6:10-24 for example) and rewrite it to themselves. Or have small groups compose a letter to the whole youth group, evaluating what the youth group is or is not doing. (Contributed by Kris Yotter, Glendale, California)

PERSONALITY PIT

This game can help your youth group get better acquainted. First of all have each person list one thing about themselves in each of the following categories:

Age
Year in School
Height
Hobby
Career aspirations
Favorite summer activity
Favorite sport
Name

Then have someone print on blank playing cards (available through many educational materials publishers) one category and response. Make sure the cards represent all of the answers given by your group.

Then shuffle and deal out the cards. The object of the game is to assemble one personality (all seven traits) by trading cards with others. Any number of cards can be traded at one time, but must be exchanged for the same number of cards in return (just like the commercial game of Pit). Play continues until someone collects all the cards which they believe describes one person in the group. The person whose personality was being described is then given a chance to confirm or deny the information. (Contributed by Joyce Fifield, St. Paul, Minnesota)

PERSONALIZED PSALMS

This is a great method of worship or meditation that is very effective. Here's how it goes:

Sit down with a Psalm—many of which lend themselves to this kind of creative meditation. Read through the Psalm several times. Each time try to identify yourself with the feeling and emotions related in the Psalm.

Put yourself into it as much as you can. Begin feeling the mood of the Psalm. As you begin feeling the emotion of the Psalm, identify these emotions with some experiences, attitudes and circumstances of your own life. Then express yourself to the Lord by writing a Psalm of your own using the original Psalm as a pattern or guideline.

If your group really gets into this method, they might want to start their own notebook of personalized Psalms. (Contributed by Dwight Scott, Ukiah, California)

PIGEON

Select a "pigeon" from the group and have them leave the room. The leader then explains to the group that they are to request of the pigeon that he/she accomplish a simple task without the benefit of verbal communication. The task can be anything reasonable, such as sitting in a chair and taking off one shoe, or lifting a coke bottle above one's head, etc. The pigeon returns to the room and stands in the center of a circle where the group is seated on the floor. The pigeon is told that he/she is to accomplish a simple task in the shortest time possible. Now, the group is instructed to clap (briskly) when the pigeon moves in a desired direction. For example: Suppose that the pigeon is instructed to take off his shoe. When the pigeon experiments (that is moves to the left, right, forward, backward, etc.) he should receive no reinforcement, no clapping from the group. Eventually, he will experiment with sitting down, standing, etc. When he begins to sit, the group will clap briskly. When he touches his shoe (which will occur eventually) the clapping will intensify. In a matter of two to three minutes the pigeon will remove his shoe. (Note: remember undesired responses receive no clapping.) This is a fascinating experiment which vividly illustrates B. F. Skinner's notion of positive reinforcement and behavior modification. This is an excellent "kick off" to a discussion regarding manipulation. (Contributed by Robert Lively, Dallas, Texas)

POLAROID CHRISTMAS TREE

If your youth group has a Christmas Tree, you might try this very rewarding idea. Take a picture of each person in your youth group. (If you don't have a polaroid camera, then have the kids bring a picture of themselves). Have them glue their picture on a small paper plate, punch a hole in the top and put in a piece of yarn to hang the ornament. Then have them decorate the plate with crayons, magic markers, and whatever else you can provide. On the back of the plate have the kids write down a Christmas wish. Hang the "ornaments" on the tree and encourage the kids to read the wishes written on each others "ornaments". (Contributed by Charles Wiltrout, New Lebanon, Ohio)

POOLING RESOURCES GAME

The following is a simple simulation which teaches the value of working together and pooling resources to accomplish a task. First, distribute a "tinker toys" game to the group, giving each person an equal number of parts. Then ask each person to make something. Many will find it difficult due to lack of adequate parts. (Each person should only receive a half dozen or so.)

Next, get them into groups of from four to ten. Have each group make something with their tinker toys brought together by the members of the group. When the groups are finished, allow them to describe their creations with everyone.

Then, discuss what happened. Was it easier to make something alone or together with others? Why? What does this tell us about bringing our resources together for a common cause? What happened in the group? What kind of process went on in the decision-making? (Contributed by Charles Stewart, Orlando, Florida)

PROBLEM HOT LINE

Have the group sit in a circle with two chairs back to back in the center of the circle. Choose two people; one to be the Hotline worker, the other a caller with a problem. The worker leaves the room while the group leader assigns a problem to the caller. When the worker returns, the caller pretends to call the worker and explain his problem. It is important that the worker and caller remain back to back. The group leader is responsible for cutting the mock call off at the proper time and leading a discussion among the rest of the group as to how the problem might be solved. Some examples of problems:

1. I am not very attractive. People avoid me and I can tell that most of the people I know make fun of me behind my back. Frankly, I'm ugly. I know it and so does everyone else. So what can I do?

2. My parents make me go to church. I like the youth program, but the worship service is a drag. Our minister is irrelevant and boring and the services don't relate to me at all.

3. My mother is dying of cancer. Every day I am faced with cancer's ugly and depressing toll on my mom. I am forced to accept more and more of her responsibilities at home. But I like to go out with my friends too. I feel guilty when I go somewhere and have a good time, but if I stay home I get angry and frustrated. What's

the answer?

4. I have always been told that kids who smoke grass and drink really don't enjoy it. So I have refrained from doing those things partly because I believed that and partly because I didn't think it was a Christian thing to do. At least until a few weeks ago. I have tried pot and drinking and it was great. I never had so much fun in my life. How can something so good be bad? Were the people who told me how bad these things were lying?

(Contributed by Tom Grove, Florence, South Carolina)

RANDOM HUNGER

This idea can be used at a camp or at any church activity where a meal is to be served. Let the group know that the meal is going to be an "experimental" situation in which the food is divided according to the world population. For a group of 100 people, the food would be divided this way:

> United States: Six people (60% of the food)
> Europe/Middle East: Sixteen people (20% of the food)
> Africa: Ten people
> South America: Eight people
> Asia (China, India): Sixty people

Africa, South America, and Asia gets the balance of the food (20%). Before the meal is served, label each table according to continents—one color for each. Cut paper squares (colors match tables) for each person in that continent. Then put all the squares in a basket and let people choose a color as they come in the door and find the table that matches. Then distribute the food and let whatever happens happen. The result can be a discussion of what went on, and the present world situation. Do not interfere with the process unless absolutely necessary.

RECYCLED HYMNS

Have your group go through your church hymnal and choose their favorite hymns. Then spend a meeting or two rewriting the words. Mimeograph the best ones and sing in your youth meetings or with the adults in the main service. These recycled hymns might become so well liked that they become a regular part of your worship. (Contributed by Marja Coons, Albuquerque, New Mexico.)

RESPONSIVE LORD'S PRAYER

The Lord's Prayer is repeated so many times in church that its meaning is often overlooked or lost altogether. The following responsive reading is designed to cause people to think more about the meaning of the Lord's Prayer as it is being recited in worship.

Leader: Our Father

People: a real person, who cares for and loves me

Leader: Who art in heaven

People: living higher than I am, understanding more than I

Leader: Hallowed be thy name

People: we honor and praise your holy name

Leader: Thy kingdom come

People: yes, come quickly Lord Jesus, live in our lives

Leader: Thy will be done

People: you always know what is best for us

Leader: On earth as it is in heaven

People: as you always have and always will

Leader: Give us this day our daily bread

People: you have always supplied our needs

Leader: And forgive us our debts

People: in the name of Christ

Leader: As we forgive our debtors

People: seventy times seven, Lord

Leader: And lead us not into temptation

People: give us the strength to resist

Leader: But deliver us from evil

People: when we fail, you come through

Leader: For thine is the kingdom

People: in which we share

Leader: and the power

People: greater than anything we have ever known

Leader: And the glory

People:	brighter than the sun
Leader:	Forever
People:	for all time to come
Leader:	Amen!
People:	Amen!

(Contributed by Donald M. Topp, Sacramento, Calif.)

ROLE BOWL

Print up the following situations on cards and put them in a bowl. Let each person in a small group pick one out and think about it. Ask the kids to share their solutions to the situation. (The more verbal kids will obviously share first. *But don't force anyone to share!*) After each person finishes, allow others in the group to comment or add their own thoughts.

1. "I don't get it". If Christianity is true, how come there are so many religions that call themselves Christian? I mean, what's the difference between Baptists, Presbyterians, etc.

2. If you ask me, the Christian religion makes you a "doormat". Always loving and turning the other cheek stuff.

3. What if I lived like hell for eighty years and then became a Christian on my death bed? Would me and Billy Graham go to the same place?

4. I have been reading through the Old Testament for English class. How come God ordered his people to kill everybody — even women and children — when they conquered a land? What kind of a God is that?

5. Your mother and I do not believe in all this Jesus stuff and we think you spend too much time in church. So we want you to stay away from church for awhile.

6. If God is God, then how come you can't see him or it? Why don't you prove that God exists? Go ahead . . . prove it to me.

7. The Bible has some nice little stories in it, but everyone knows it's full of contradictions, errors and just plain myths. How can you believe it?

8. I know a bunch of people that go to your church and they are supposed to be Christians, but I also know what they do during the week and at parties that I go to. They are phonies. If Christianity is so great, how come so many phonies?

9. My little brother died of leukemia and I prayed like crazy. Don't tell me there is a God who loves us. How come he didn't help my brother?

10. Look, I know I am overweight and even though it hurts me to say it, I'm ugly. And I started coming to your church because I

thought the kids in your youth group would treat me differently than the kids do at school. Wrong! They ignore me and make fun of me just like everyone else. How come?

(Contributed by Bob Stier, New Providence, New Jersey)

ROUTINE AND HUMDRUM

Read the parable below to your group and then discuss. Here are some suggestions for questions to get you started:

1. Shouldn't life be exciting for the Christian?
2. Isn't routine and stability the opposite of creativity and growth?
3. Is there anything wrong with not working?
4. Is it wrong to want excitement?
5. What does it mean to be faithful?
6. If our church is boring and unfulfilling, should we stick it out or look for a church that is more fulfilling?

A Parable

There landed on my Doorstep a Damsel. And ere I could Greet her, she spake unto me, "Is not Life so Exciting." For she had been Traveling Here and There, stopping only to Visit with Other Believers.

Musing, I enquired of the Damsel, "How doth the Excitement of Life Manifest Itself?" Then did she Beam. "There are So Many new people to Meet. And the Lord doth Supply all my Need."

"How doth He so?" I wondered, "Seeing thou dost Remain in One Place not so long as to Obtain Regular Employment."

Again she spake in Glowing Terms. "Do not Believers everywhere Take Me In? For that is the way with Christians. Yea, and I am Helpful and do Exciting Things."

And I bethought me of Life, and of those who are the Faithful in the Church. Yea, and Especially of those Elders who Every Day for Twenty Years and more go Five Days a Week to the Same Job. Yet they Give Attention to the Care of the Flock, Day after Day, Year after Year.

"But what of Those," I asked, "who must each Day care for a Home and Children regularly and continually?" And her reply was, "Oh, that is so Humdrum."

Then did I take Note that Life is for Most of Us Routine. Indeed, Chaos would Result if we Demanded Excitement. Even would the Church Itself fall Apart. For Order and Comfort depend upon Routine and Stability. It was Solomon who had Tried All Novelty, who said, "Behold, what I have seen to be good and to be fitting is to eat and drink and find enjoyment in all the toil with which one toils under the sun the few days of his life which God has given him."

So to the Damsel I spake these words in Parting, "Thou has not yet Grown Up."

RUN FOR YOUR LIFE

Although this strategy deals with the subject of death, it is really about life and how we live it. The purpose of this exercise is to help young people to evaluate their priorities in light of what is really important. It allows the group to contrast what they are doing now with what they would do if they only had one month to live. Give each person in the group a list similar to the one below:

If I only had one month to live, I would:

1. Perform some high risk feat that I have always wanted to do, figuring that if I don't make it, it won't really matter.
2. Stage an incredible robbery for a large amount of money which I would immediately give to the needy and starving of the world.
3. Not tell anyone.
4. Use my dilemma to present the gospel to as many people as I could.
5. Spend all my time in prayer and Bible reading.
6. Make my own funeral arrangements.
7. Offer myself to science or medicine to be used for experiments that might have fatal results.
8. Have as much fun as possible (sex, parties, booze, whatever turns me on.)
9. Travel around the world and see as much as possible.
10. Buy lots of stuff on credit that I've always wanted: expensive cars, fancy clothes, exotic food, etc. ("Sorry, the deceased left no forwarding address.")
11. Spend my last month with my family or close personal friends.
12. Not do anything much different. Just go on as always.
13. Isolate myself from everyone, find a remote place and meditate.
14. Write a book about my life (or last month).
15. Sell all my possessions and give the money to my family, friends, or others who need it.
16. Try to accomplish as many worthwhile projects as possible.
17. _____

Have the group rank these alternatives (plus any they wish to add) from first to last choice. The first item on their list would be the one they would probably do, and the last would be the one they would probably not do. Have everyone share their choices, explain why they chose that way, and then discuss the results with the entire group. Another way to evaluate the alternatives is to put each one on a continuum. On one end of the continuum would be "Yes, definitely" and on the other end, "Absolutely not." After each alternative is placed on the continuum, compare and discuss with the rest of the group.

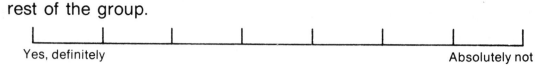

Yes, definitely   Absolutely not

(Contributed by John Boller, Jr., San Diego, California)

SANTA'S BIRTHDAY PARTY

Around Christmas time plan a birthday party for someone in the youth group (Depending on the person, it might be best to clue them in as to what you are doing). Use a lot of publicity and include the fact that Santa will be appearing at the party with gifts for everyone. Each person that attends the party is to bring a gift for the birthday person and one other gift.

Although the party is supposed to be a birthday party, do everything you can to emphasize Santa's appearance. Hang signs that say "Welcome Santa", put the Christmas tree with gifts in a central location. The Happy Birthday signs and cake should be small and off to the side.

At the party play some games, sing and while you are singing "happy birthday" to the birthday person, have Santa appear with surprises and gifts for everyone. Make a big deal out of Santa's appearance with picture taking and kids sitting on Santa's lap.

After Santa leaves and there is a pause then remember the birthday person and have them open their gifts.

At the end of the get together discuss what took place. What happened to the birthday person? How did they feel when Santa got all the attention? Would you want to be the one for whom the party was given? (Contributed by Dave Gilliam, Grove, Oklahoma)

SCREWTAPE LETTERS

This exercise is a good way to make the kids think about a topic by coming in through the back door. Divide them into groups of about five kids each and assign a recorder who is given pen and paper. Explain to the kids what a "Screwtape Letter" is and if you own the book (*Screwtape Letters* by C. S. Lewis), read a few excerpts so that they get the idea. Next, have them write a Screwtape Letter on "How To Destroy a Christian's Prayer Life" or a similar topic. In the process, they must consider what makes a good prayer life before they can write down how to destroy it. If you want, you can have them first of all list five or ten things necessary for a good prayer life and then work on those. Most kids love to show how devious they can be anyway, and in the process of being devious and creative, they have to consider what constitutes an effective prayer life. Have each group read theirs and then discuss. (Contributed by Len Carlson, Hopkins, Minnesota)

THE SECRET

Mr. and Mrs. Benjamin are close friends with Bob and Lisa Sanders. Both couples are long time members of the same church, pastored by Rev. Evans.

All three couples are having dinner at the Benjamin's house Saturday night. A few days before the dinner, while Mrs. Benjamin is out shopping, she notices a commotion at the exit. Apparently, someone was being stopped for shoplifting. To Mrs. Benjamin's amazement that someone is Lisa Sanders. Shocked and embarrassed, Mrs. Benjamin darted out of the store not knowing whether Lisa saw her or not.

Mrs. Benjamin feels very close to Lisa and plans to discuss the matter privately with her. But she is worried that such a discussion might damage their relationship.

Mr. Benjamin does not think his wife should mention it and believes it should be forgotten.

Bob Sanders has no idea his wife is shoplifting and the knowledge of such would be humiliating to him and he would have a difficult time understanding or forgiving.

Lisa Sanders knows that Mrs. Benjamin saw her and wants desperately to get help from her friends but is afraid her husband, Bob, could not handle it.

Rev. Evans is totally unaware of Lisa Sanders' problem.

Mrs. Evans has a difficult time accepting that Christians sin. Especially something like shoplifting.

The Situation: Just as the three couples sit down for dessert, a teenage son of the Benjamin's runs in saying loudly, "Hey, mom, Sonny just told me that Mrs. Sanders got arrested for shoplift—" (*he suddenly sees Mr. and Mrs. Sanders*).

Have those chosen to act out this role play react to this situation. When you feel enough has been said, stop the role play and discuss what happened. Ask the role players to discuss what they were feeling and then get comment from the group. (Contributed by Bruce Otto, Vancouver, B.C. Canada)

THE SERMON OF THE MOUSE

The following article can be read aloud to the group or it can be printed and passed out to each person. It raises some important issues concerning the church and should be discussed using the questions that follow or others that you may want to add.

The Sermon of the Mouse

The day had finally arrived. Everyone in the congregation was waiting expectantly. The negotiations had taken months, but finally everything had been worked out. It wasn't every congregation in the country that could have an opportunity like this. It was a rare visit from a very well known celebrity.

The pastor and his guest mounted the platform. The first hymn was sung. Then the pastor rose, "I'm sure everyone is aware who our guest speaker is this morning," he said.

Aware? How could anyone help being aware? There were posters all over town. There was a big yellow and black banner stretched across the entry to the parking lot. Seating in the sanctuary had been done on a reservation basis with preferential treatment given to members in good standing of the congregation. An overflow crowd was watching the service on closed circuit television. Everybody knew about it.

"It isn't often," said the pastor, "that we have an opportunity to meet someone who has become a legend in his own time. Starting back in the bleak years of the depression with a shoe string budget and a very simple plan, our guest, with hard work and contagious enthusiasm, built an empire for himself that rivals that of Howard Hughes. His name is a household word, he is admired by young and old alike, and he has even survived his mentor. He reigns over a multi-million dollar business venture that was so successful in Southern California that he established an even more spectacular venture in Florida. By now, I'm sure you know who I am talking about. We are so honored to have Mickey Mouse with us today to share with us the secrets of Disneyland's success with the hope that our church will be stimulated and helped by his story."

A hush came over the congregation as this famous mouse rose to his feet, cleared his throat, and began his sermon.

"Thank you for inviting me to come to your church. I must admit at first I was surprised that a church would ask me to give a sermon. Oh, I have been invited to Sunday School contests where they give each new person a Mickey Mouse Hat and expect me to shake hands with everyone and act funny, but a sermon is something new.

"But after I thought about it, I realized that maybe Disneyland and the church did have a lot in common and as I began to organize my thoughts, I saw how ingenious it was to invite me to share. I really believe that if your church were to apply our principles you could become as successful as Disneyland.

"First. Make sure your enterprise seems exciting, even dangerous, but be quick to let your people know that there really is no danger involved. *Give the illusion of great risk,* but make sure everything is perfectly safe.

"Second, admit that you are in the entertainment business. People won't care what you say as long as they're entertained. Keep your people happy. Don't tell them anything negative. And don't make demands on them. Just keep them diverted from the ugly reality of today's world and they will keep coming back for more.

"Third, make everything look religious. Make the religious experience so elaborate, so intricate, so complex that only the professionals can pull it off and all the laymen can do is stand around with their mouths open and watch. People would rather watch an imitation mechanical bird sing than they would a real bird anyway. They would rather watch worship than do it.

"Fourth and finally, pretend that there are no problems. At Disneyland we dress our security guards up as smiling rabbits or friendly bears because we don't want anyone's experience at Disneyland to be ruined by the sight of law enforcement personnel. Disguise your problems and failures behind a warm smile and a firm handshake. Leave them at home and let the church be a happy place where there aren't any ugly problems. Just friendly pastors and smiling deacons.

"People today want good clean entertainment. They want an environment that is safe for children and they want a place that is safe for their family and friends. I am so glad to see that the church is moving in this direction. Thank you and God bless you."

Questions for discussion:

1. What parallels, if any, do you see between Disneyland and the organized church?

2. Analyze each of the mouse's points. Below are some questions that may help:

"Give the illusion of great risk, but make everything safe."

a. Are there any risks involved in being a Christian today?

b. Does modern Christianity really cost the Christian anything?

c. Can you think of any examples of the church creating an "illusion" of risk?

d. How, if at all, does a church make people "safe"?

"Entertain the people."

a. How do churches "entertain" their people?

b. Should Christianity and the church be entertaining?

c. React to this statement: "People today must be entertained. After all, they have become sophistocated by watching the professional entertainment on television and at the movies. The church is competing for a person's time and attention and must give them something to make them want to come. After they get there, then they can be given spiritual content.

"Make everything look religious."

a. Define "religious."

b. What do you think Mickey Mouse meant by "religious"?

"Pretend there are no problems."

a. Do you think the church should admit to having problems? The pastor? The people?

b. How can a church pretend it doesn't have any problems?

c. If Christianity is true, then don't problems raise doubts in the minds of searching unbelievers?

(Story contributed by Dave Phillips, Old Greenwich, Connecticut)

SHOES OF CHRIST

Here's an idea that can be used to illustrate the meaning behind Paul's concept of the uniqueness of each member within the Body of Christ. Have the kids sit in a circle, remove their shoes and place them in the middle of the circle. Talk about the features that shoes have in common and then discuss what makes each pair unique. Then have the kids take a pair of someone else's shoes and attempt to put them on. They will soon discover how difficult it is to wear someone else's shoes. Return everyone's shoes and discuss what it means to be unique in the Body of Christ. (Contributed by Van Edington, Marietta, Georgia)

SHOW AND TELL

Invite each person in your group to bring a personal object that represents something about their feelings about life. They could bring anything including trophies, books, pictures, mementoes, etc.) After the person shares what he or she brought with the group, then others in the group may ask questions. When everyone has shared, the leader then asks: 1) What new things did you learn about the people who shared? 2) What did you each learn about yourselves? (Contributed by Don Highlander, Stone Mountain, Georgia)

SINGING WORSHIP SERVICE

This is an attempt to put more meaning into the songs we sing in church. Have the kids (one at a time) request favorite songs. The only condition to singing it is that the kid must give a personally meaningful reason for requesting that particular song. (Contributed by Ron Wilburn, El Paso, Texas)

SOLOMON'S COLLAGE

Conduct a study of Ecclesiastes 2 which describes Solomon's vain experimentation with pleasure (sex, entertainment, alcohol), possessions (homes, lands, wealth), and even the accumulation of wisdom and knowledge. This can be compared with how modern advertising still tries to convince the public that these same things are the "answer" to life and the pursuit of happiness. Distribute magazines, scissors, marking pens, and glue to the group and have them compose collages using advertisements and quotes from the scripture text to communicate what they learned. This can result in a very impressive and thought-provoking display for the church lobby or youth meeting room. (Contributed by Ron Rosenau, Charlotte, Michigan)

SPIRITUAL GIFT LIST

Make a list of all the "gifts of the spirit" found in Ephesians 4, I Corinthians 12, and Romans 12. Then have everyone in the group "rank order" the gifts from most important to least important and explain why they made their choices. Then discuss in light of Paul's advice in I Cor. 12:3 1 to "earnestly desire the greater gifts."

THE TATOR FAMILY

Here is an idea that can (and has) been used in a number of ways - from bulletin inserts to sermons, plays and skits. However it is used, it is a clever and rather entertaining way to illustrate both the positive and negative aspects of common traits found in people.

Here are the members of the "Tator" family:

1. *Speck Tator:* He likes to watch everyone else rather than get involved in anything personally. He is always on the outside looking in. He is usually expert at evaluating and helps those who are participating by cheering them on. But because Speck has the advantage of watching from the stands, he can also make unrealistic assessments from a distance and be quite fickle with his support.

2. *Dick Tator:* Dick doesn't consult anyone. He makes all his decisions by himself and sees others only as means to accomplish his will. Dick usually gets high marks for getting things done, but low marks for working with others.

3. *Agi Tator:* Whenever things get dull, Agi is always there to stir things up. She is often a nuisance, but many times keeps everyone on their toes by disturbing the comfortable status quo.

4. *Hesi Tator:* It is very difficult for Hesi to make decisions. She always needs just a little bit more information before making a decision. If and when Hesi does make a decision, however, it has usually been thought through carefully.

5. *Emmy Tator:* Emmy is a follower and can easily become a hero worshiper. Heavily influenced by those around her, Emmy's future is determined by the kinds of people she patterns her life after.

6. *Common Tator:* Common always has advice or criticism on any subject. Always talking and always very authoritative sounding, he often sounds like he knows what he is talking about, but usually doesn't.

7. *Irri Tator:* Irri is a twin of Agi with a mean streak in her. She likes to stir things up just for the sake of causing confusion and disarray. She is abrasive and even when she takes the correct position on a subject, still winds up alienating those around her.

8. *Vegi Tator:* Some call Vegi lazy because she just sits around doing nothing. She doesn't take any risks and tends to take what's given without giving anything in return. But at least Vegi is predictable and somewhat stable.

9. *Devis Tator:* Devis is a revolutionary. He believes in confrontation, radical change. It is his philosophy that the only way to change something is to destroy it and start all over. Devis is weak on alternatives or ideas for rebuilding, but considers that someone else's job.

10. *Facili Tator:* Facili is warm and personable. She is almost selfless. She works hard at enabling others to become better. She is a good listener and asks the kinds of questions that allow people to speak about things that matter to them. But Facili can sometimes be a nuisance because she sees every gathering as an opportunity to use her gifts and sometimes she just needs to let her abilities remain dormant.

11. *Cogi Tator:* Cogi is a thinker. She is different from her brother Medi, in that Cogi thinks deeply about matters that will affect the way she acts. She weighs everything carefully before acting and attempts to make sure she has considered all the alternatives.

12 *Medi Tator:* Medi thinks deeply and finds satisfaction in the act itself. His thinking never really leads to any constructive action, however. It is the act of pondering that matters to Medi and not the content.

13. *Roe Tator:* Roe is a systems man. He believes that everyone should have their turn regardless of qualification. He is task oriented and is only involved as long as the task is his responsibility. He believes in change for change's sake and doesn't like to remain in one spot too long.

(Contributed by Kenneth Jacobsen, San Diego, California)

TEN YEARS FROM NOW

Here's a fun discussion starter for junior highers (and others, for that matter). Print the following on a half sheet of paper and let the kids answer away. Don't have them put their name on the paper (if your group is shy) and discuss them as a group. If your kids don't mind sharing their responses then simply go around the group and discuss each one individually.

```
                     TEN YEARS FROM NOW...

       1. My height  _____
       2. My weight  _____
       3. My hair style  _____
       4. Where I will be living  _____
       5. What I will be doing  _____
       6. Dreams and Goals I will have  _____
       7. I FEEL I WILL HAVE BEEN A SUCCESS IN LIFE IF . . .


       8. I WILL LOOK BACK UPON THIS YEAR AS A YEAR OF . . .
```

(Contributed by Pat and Ray Hilwig, Marblehead, Massachusetts)

THIS LITTLE BITE OF MINE

This is an interesting discussion starter on the subject of love. Read the story below to your group:

> I heard a story about a man who was bitten by a dog. When the health officer tested the dog, sure enough, it was rabid. As soon as the victim heard this, he grabbed a pad of paper and a pen and began writing as fast as he could.
>
> "Hey, we can give you a serum, you know. You don't have to write out your will," said the health officer.
>
> "Oh, I'm not writing my will," cried the bitten man. I'm making a list of all the people I want to bite."

After reading the story, give your young people these instructions:

1. Put yourself in this man's place. Pretend that you have been bitten by a rabid dog and make a list of five people you want to bite. Include a one or two word note by each name to remind you why you want to bite them. Leave an inch or so of space below each name.

2. Now turn this around. Act as if you were afflicted by the infectious disease of love. List five people you would like to bite now. Make a note to remind you why and leave an inch below each name.

3. Now discuss what happened. Are any of the people on both lists? Why? Can you feel hate for someone and still love them? Is it possible to consciously love someone? In other words, if you calculate loving someone, is that love? If you have to tell someone you love them, do you really love them?

(Contributed by Randy Dillard, Burlington, North Carolina)

THE TIE THAT BINDS

Have all the kids stand in a circle. Any group up to thirty will work. Take a long thick piece of rope or cord and loop it around each kid as in the following illustration. Be sure there is no slack between

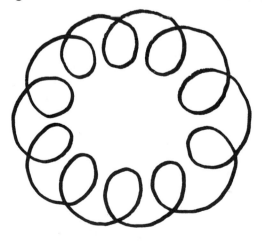

them, and have them move close together. With no explanation of the purpose or point, have each kid take a large step backwards one at a time. Go all the way around the circle. (Normally, someone about halfway around will get the bright idea to give a good squeeze to the ones next to him; allow this.) When everyone has stepped back, have them drop the rope and sit down.

Discuss two things: what happened when you stepped back (to you and the ones around you), and what happened when the persons next to you stepped back, and what part did the rope play in this experience?

Now talk about the "tie that binds" in John 13:35, our love for one another. One observation that comes across clearly is: When someone tries to break from fellowship, our love as a group should always hold him in. Close by singing, "Blest Be the Tie That Binds." (Contributed by Steven Robinson, Lubbock, Texas)

TINKER TOY GAME

The following experiment can be used with either adult youth sponsors or with kids. When used with sponsors, it can demonstrate to them the advantages of allowing kids to discover truth on their own. With kids, it will help them to see the value in using their head rather than always wanting to be "spoon-fed."

First, divide your group into small groups of four or five. Then give each group a box of tinker toys with the instructions, "Make something that works." Insist that each person has a say in the project. They will really have a good time with this, so be patient. When the masterpieces are completed, ask each group to explain what they have.

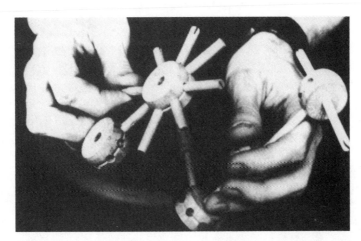

Second, line everyone up in a single line. Scatter the tinker toys evenly throughout the line. Now you are the director and you guide them piece by piece to build a simple structure with the tinker toys. (For example: "Take the red pieces and fit them into this round

139

piece like this....") It doesn't matter what you make. Keep it simple. What matters is that you don't let anyone get ahead of the group. If they put the piece in before you tell them, get mad or call them down. (The results will be that they have a tendency to get childish. That doesn't matter. Just make them go step by step as you instruct them.) When you finish, go around the line and have them tell you what they have. Everyone will give a different answer, but you inform them that they can't tell you what they have because you are the one who made it and only you know what it is.

Third, it's time for discussion. Again, be sensitive to your own group and its special needs as you discuss. The two experiments represent two ways of teaching. The first is guiding the student to come up with something on his own that works. It is his and he has ownership in it. The second represents cramming your beliefs, prejudices, or opinions down the throat of the student. Ask your people which way they preferred, and have them give reasons why. (Contributed by Larry Jansen, Indianapolis, Indiana)

TOE PAINTING

Here is an idea that will allow everyone to creatively express themselves in an unusual way. Prior to the meeting, the group should be instructed that they are to come with extra clean feet. In addition, it will helpful if they bring a towel. These instructions generally arouse questions and generate a good response because the group wants to know why such weird orders. They soon find out. When the group has gathered, they are instructed to take off all shoes and socks and to roll up their pant legs several inches. The reason why is they are going to "toe-paint." And all that is is finger painting, only you stand up and let your toes do the work.

All painting materials have been gathered together ahead of time and have been placed in an area where water is handy and where no damage will occur should a few painted footprints touch the floor.

The toe-paintings can be done individually or the group can combine toe talents and paint a mural.

First, here is what could happen when you do it on an individual basis. Select a general theme such as "Show What God Means to You Today," and have the young people express their feelings about this theme by toe-painting. After the group has finished painting, form a circle in some other part of the church and allow each person to share his or her painting with the group by telling in words what feelings they painted.

To paint a mural, sheets of finger-painting paper are taped together prior to the meeting. Again a general theme is selected, such as

"Christmas." The mural can then be divided into three parts and the young people can select the section they wish to paint in. One third of the mural might show the wise men and their camels heading toward Bethlehem. The middle section could show the stable with the Christ child in a manger. The last section would show the shepherds watching over their flocks. After the mural is finished (and dried, of course) it is hung so that it can be appreciated by all.

No matter what way you choose to use toe-painting, it is helpful, and fun, to have a poloroid camera ready to take pictures of your toe-painting process. These pictures are also displayed along with the finished paintings. Some people will find it hard to believe that your group really painted with toes because the quality of art is really pretty good. The pictures of the process bear witness that you really put your foot into it. (Contributed by Earl H. Estill, Gainesville, Texas)

TOM MEETS GOD

Here's a short skit with a message. It requires three players, and should be well rehearsed before presentation to the group. Follow up the skit with a discussion of what happened. Although this skit is quite short, there are several issues raised worth getting into.

TOM: *(Knocks and an "angel" opens the door)* Hi! My name is Tom. I would like to see the person in charge, please.

ANGEL: Sure, come on in.

TOM: Look, aaa, I know this guy is really important, but do you think he would see someone like me.

ANGEL: He sees everyone. You can see him any time you'd like.

TOM: Could I see him now?

ANGEL: Go right on in.

TOM: Now?

ANGEL: Yes.

TOM *(Hesitating and then slowly walks in)* Uh, excuse me, my name is Tom. I wondered if I could see you for a few minutes?

GOD: My name is God and I've got all the time you need.

TOM: Well, I'm going to high school right now, and I am a little confused about what I should do... A couple of my friends say you can help, but they seem just as confused as I am. To be quite honest, I haven't really been impressed by your work. I mean, don't get me wrong, my friends are really good friends, you know, and they really seem to like me, but, they haven't got it so good. Bob, one of my friends, has a dad that is an alcoholic and my other friend's folks are getting a divorce. The crazy thing is my folks are great, I really love them, everything's going great

... except ... except I can't seem to see the point in life. In spite of all the junk that is happening to my friends, they really seem to be convinced that you are important. So that's why I'm here. I just thought you could give me some pointers. I just feel kinda lost.

GOD: My price is high.

TOM: That's ok, because my folks are pretty well off. What is it?

GOD: All.

TOM: All?

GOD: Yes, All. Everything.

TOM: Sheesh. Don't you have a lay-a-way plan? How about a pay as you go. Isn't your profit margin a little out of line?

GOD: Actually, my cost was quite high also ... ask my Son.

TOM: Well, a, I think I'll have to wait awhile. I appreciate you're taking the time to talk to me and I'm sure you're worth it, it's just that at my age, It's a little too soon to give up everything. After all, when you're young that's when the good times happen. Besides, I think I can get what I'm looking for at a much cheaper price.

GOD: Be careful, Tom. The price may be cheaper, but your cost may be much higher than you think.

TOM: Yeah, sure. Well, nice talking to you, God. Maybe, I'll see you around some time.

GOD: Yes, Tom, and there's no maybe about it.

(Adapted from an idea contributed by Abiding Savior Lutheran Church, Scottsdale, Arizona)

TORTOISE AND THE HARE

This is a fun little discussion starter that could serve as an icebreaker in a larger discussion on the importance of each person in the Body of Christ.

Give your group two categories such as "Turtles" and "Rabbits." Ask them to decide which of the two categories they would rather be. Those that decide to be turtles go to one side of the room and rabbits go to the other side of the room. Then have each group discuss why they chose their category and make a list of their reasons. Then have a volunteer from each group read back their list of reasons. Combine everyone into one group again and give two new categories, repeating the entire process. Here are some suggestions for categories:

Volkswagon - Cadillac
River - Lake
Multimillionaire - President
Black - Oriental
Tall - Short

You can come up with many other categories. After you have done this exercise a number of times, bring the group together and discuss the problems of accepting people's circumstances and learning to accept our own circumstances. (Contributed by Scott Wilson, Dallas, Texas)

TOUR OF YOUR LIFE

This day-long field trip is great with junior highs and gives them an opportunity to view life somewhat more completely and realistically. Begin by visiting the maternity ward of a local hospital (pre-arranged, of course) where the kids can see newborns and their parents. Perhaps a doctor can tell about the birth process and give a brief tour of the area. Next, take the kids to a local college or university campus, and show them around. The next stop should be a factory or shop where people are at work. At this point, the need for work and the types of work available can be discussed. Then proceed to a convalescent home or some other place where senior citizens live and visit with the older folks. Allow the kids to share with them in some way and allow the seniors to also share with the kids in some way. The last stop on the tour should be a mortuary or funeral home. The funeral director may show the kids around, explain what happens to the body when it is brought in; the types of caskets available, and so on. Close the experience with a meeting or discussion in the funeral chapel (if there is one) or elsewhere if you wish. Other places can be added to this tour depending on how much time you have or the types of places available to you. Allow kids to think about their own lives, the kind of life that they want, and how they are going to achieve their goals.

TRANSLATING THE LORD'S PRAYER

Whether your group is too familiar with the Lord's Prayer or unfamiliar with it, this is a great exercise that will not only familiarize them with the Lord's Prayer, but help them to understand some of its deepest meanings.

1. By using any one of numerous available sources (Concordance, Bible Dictionary, Good News For Modern Man Index), locate the two passages in the New Testament that contain the Lord's Prayer. Discuss the similarities and differences between Matthew's (Matthew 6:9-13) and Luke's (Luke 11:2-4) versions.

2. Distribute as many translations of the New Testament that you have available (suggestions: Revised Standard, American Standard, Phillips, New English, Today's English, Moffatt). Have the young people read aloud from at least three different versions.

3. Have the students individually compose and write their own version of the Lord's Prayer using any or all the translations available. They may select the words and phrases of each verse they feel most effective or meaningful.

4. After each person has finished, have them share their Lord's Prayer "translation" with the others in the group.

5. By consensus or voting, compose a group "translation" of the Lord's Prayer that best conveys the group's understanding of the prayer.

The group "translation" could then be used in the regular worship service accompanied by a very meaningful explanation by the group as to how and why they composed their prayer the way they did. (Contributed by Kenneth Cramer, Bellefonte, Pennsylvania)

TV CHRISTMAS STORY

Here is a dramatic presentation that can be given at Christmas time centered around a Television newscast. The newscast occurs on the first Christmas day but is done with a modern set. Simply reproduce a large TV News set complete with monitor, station call letters in the back, etc. You could even go so far as to construct phony cameras, etc. All of the news commentators should be dressed in modern clothes. Feel free to adapt, add to or subtract any part of the script you want.

SCRIPT:

ANN: Stay tuned for the VBS Evening News with Barnabas Cronkite with the latest on a strange sighting in the sky; Martha Waltersberg from downtown Bethlehem where a huge crowd is gathering for the tax enrollment, Dr. Ben Hadad with reports about a new cold front moving in. That's the VBS news coming up next.

COMM: Taxes. Taxes. Taxes. No one likes to pay taxes. Especially when H & R Blockberg can help you pay the least taxes possible. H & R Blockberg is the only tax consulting service authorized by the Roman Government and each and every consultant has previous tax collecting experience. Yes, you can trust H & R Blockberg for all your tax related problems. H & R Blockberg, 700 Appian Way.

ANN: The VBS Evening News with Barnabas Cronkite in Jerusalem, Martha Waltersberg in Bethlehem and Dr. Ben Hadad on Mt. Ararat. Brought to you by Hertz Donkey Rental — the Donkeys O.J. Feldman rides and Gethsemane Nurseries, with gardens in every major city. Now ... Barnabas Cronkite.

BAR: Good Evening. There has been a new development on the strange light that has been sighted in the eastern hemisphere for the last few nights. Correspondent Moshe Smith reports . . .

MOS: For the past few nights a bright light or starlike phenomena has been appearing in the sky. At first it was thought to be a meteor or an optical illusion, but tonight Dr. Ishmael Streisand confirmed that what everyone is seeing is, in fact, a star. The question is where did this star come from and what does it mean. Officials close to the situation are speculating that the star is not an isolated incident and that more strange occurances may be expected. Concerned government officials are monitoring the situation closely and reliable sources have told VBS that other incidents have not been made public. This is Correspondent Moshe Smith in Jerusalem.

BAR: VBS news has learned that an incident did occur near Bethlehem and we now switch to our mini-cam live in the hills of Bethlehem. David Saul Reports.

DAV: Barnabas, approximately ten minutes ago a group of shepherds told me that they saw some kind of an angel accompanied by music and bright lights. Normally, stories from shepherds are discounted because of the fact that they are a strange breed . . . and tend to hit the sauce . . . *but* government officials here seem strangely concerned. From my discussions with the shepherds apparently they think this has something to do with a Messiah promised years ago. The mention of the Messiah seems to be what has government officials so concerned. From the hills of Bethlehem, this has been David Saul reporting.

BAR: We'll be right back after this message from Hertz.

COM: O.J. Feldman here for Hertz.
When you're in a strange town, it's nice to know your friends at Hertz are ready to help. Maybe you had to trade in your donkey for tax money, or yours kicks people in crowds, that's the time to rent a donkey from Hertz. Our donkeys are used to crowds and are guaranteed to get you where you want to go. Of course, Hertz uses nothing but fine GMAC donkeys. Hertz — where we treat donkeys like donkeys and treat you right.

BAR: Last month Ceasar Augustus issued a decree requiring all citizens to return to the city of birth in order to attain an accurate enrollment for taxing. Martha Waltersberg is in Bethlehem for the story.

MAR: I'm standing here at the No Room Inn on the outskirts of Bethlehem. Thousands of people are swarming into the city now and every available facility is full. Just a few minutes ago a woman who is about to have a baby was almost turned away. Finally, after protests from her husband, they were allowed to stay with the animals. We just finished talking with the head of the Best Eastern Lodge Association and he suggests that anyone heading for Bethlehem attempt to find lodging outside of town. The head of the Roman Government here in Bethlehem is deeply concerned about crowd control. So far, there have not been any major incidents. The question is, can this uneasy quiet continue? Martha Waltersberg at the No Room Inn in Bethlehem.

BAR: A group of highly respected astrologers have begun a significant journey. Correspondent Mort Solomon reports from Peking.

MOR: Walter, a large party of wealthy astrologers are traveling towards Israel to observe a strange light. Apparently it is the same strange light seen over Israel the past few weeks. Informed sources have told us that these men believe there is some relation between the light and the Messiah. Although there has been no official recognition by the Roman government it is believed that when the astrologers arrive within Roman territory they will be summoned before government officials. Reporters here, Walter, are baffled as to this sudden concern on the part of Roman officials for this promised Messiah. Why, we just will have to wait and see. Mort Solomon from China.

COM: The VBS News will continue in just a moment. Ladies, now is the time to order your hooded cape and robes. The Good Hood company has an incredible selection now. These hooded capes and robes are all one piece of material and the hood cannot be lost nor can it become entangled in water jugs being carried on the head. The Good Hood Company — where we also have a clearance on beautiful sheepskin swimming suits. Come by and see us soon.

BAR: Eric Rosen has been watching with interest the increasing speculation about a coming Messiah. Eric.

ERIC: The reason there is so much concern about a Messiah, of course, is the popular notion by the Jews that such a Messiah will become a political force and overthrow the Romans. This is a hope that Jews have had for years and we have seen potential "Messiahs" come and go. We have a feeling that the strange light in the East is nothing more than a passing phenomena that those who are overly religious and mystical can cling to or, worse yet, use to mount a revolutionary movement. I have done

146

some research on this matter of a Messiah and I am not so sure that if and when such a Saviour were to appear, it would be a political leader. I am sure I will get a lot of mail about this, but I think it would be much more profitable if those who are so anxiously awaiting a Messiah would start living like they believed in the God they say they do. I guess it is always easier and less threatening to hope in the future than to live like the future were now.

Eric Rosen . . . VBS News.

BAR: Jerusalem has been the home of the National Open Spear Throwing Olympics. Stud Barjonas reports.

STUD: Coming off of major upset victories, two Hebrews will be facing each other in the finals to be held next Friday. Friday's match between Philip of Caesarea and Simion of Bethany has already been sold out. There is some concern that Philip of Caesarea may have trouble keeping his feet within the specified boundaries on his approach. He refused comment on the two warnings he received today. However, sources close to Philip confirm that he will be wearing a new imported brand of sandal to give him additional footing. Should be quite a match. In chariot racing today, Fireball Jonah narrowly escaped serious injury when his vehicle turned over in the northwest turn at the Hippodrome. This turn is considered one of the most hazardous in racing. In spite of the mishap, Jonah went on to win the main event.

BAR: Dr. Ben Hadad has been standing by on Mt. Ararat for the weather report, but we have just received a bulletin from Bethlehem. Martha Waltersberg is there.

MAR: Walter, as you know from my earlier report I am at the No Room Inn here in Bethlehem. Just as we were getting ready to leave, we were told of a commotion at the back of the inn. We found a young girl who had just given birth to a baby where they keep the animals. Normally, we would have ignored the story, but, Walter, something strange is occurring here. A huge crowd is gathering and a number of shepherds and others almost seem to be worshipping the baby. We have been unable to get any comment from anyone here, but there is one thing else. That strange light in the East seems to be much brighter now and almost seems to be directly above us. This is Martha Waltersberg in a stable in Bethlehem.

BAR: And that's the way it is. Barnabas Cronkite for the VBS Evening News. Good Night.

(Adapted from an idea contributed by Fred Davis, Denver, Colorado)

TRACT DRAFT

This can be an excellent way to discuss the significance of "gospel tracts" and at the same time help your young people understand what the gospel is.

First of all, bring a variety of sample gospel tracts for your kids to look over. You should make sure you have a variety of styles from hard core fundamentalism to denominational and fairly contemporary tracts. Discuss each of the tracts including questions like:

1. What is the purpose of tracts?
2. Is it possible for a tract to be effective? If not, why not? If so, are there any exceptions?
3. If you think it is possible to have a good tract, what criteria would you use, if any?
4. Have you ever been handed a tract? If so, what was your reaction? What was the reaction of other people?
5. Have you ever given anyone a tract? Why? What happened.

If you as a group have come to the conclusion that tracts can be used and have developed some criteria for their use, then divide up into groups (if large enough) and write your own tracts. Encourage creativity! Let them really use their imaginations. Then have the entire group evaluate each tract. (Adapted from an idea contributed by Ray Houser, Fresno, California)

TWENTY FIRST CENTURY

Future Shock is something that effects all of us, and this discussion can help your kids start preparing for the future.

Begin with a devotional on Revelation 21:1-5. Talk about what God has planned for the future: a new heaven and a new earth; no more tears; no more death; no more grief, crying or pain, etc. That's all great but what about the world we live in now? What is going to happen in the next few years?

Give each of the kids a list like the one below:

Travel/Transportation
Government
Work
Recreation
Housing/Architecture
Entertainment
Personal Items
Church
Food
Clothes
Education

Environment
Household Gadgets
Social Relations
Economy (money)

Divide into groups and have each group select areas of interest. Then give each group 45 minutes to illustrate, symbolize or fantasize the world they would like to see in the Twenty First Century. Display all the posters at the end of the session and have each group talk about their poster. (Contributed by Jimmie L. Hancock, Elmendorf AFB, Alaska)

A VERY SPECIAL BIBLE READING

So often when one simply reads a Bible reading out loud, it loses the interest of many youth. If you have ever found this to be true, then the following personal approach can really help. Instead of expecting every word to mean something to every youth, assign a special verse or verses to specific youth for personal consideration. The following reading is an adaptation of I Timothy 2:1-18.

As I read God's word tonight, I ask that you not only give attention to the entire reading, but special attention to those verses I will give to you personally. I trust that they will be extra meaningful to you.

Our Lord in his Holy Word says, _Bob_ (insert name of youth and read to him or her) "Be strong with the strength Christ Jesus gives you. For you must teach others those things you and many others have heard me speak about. Teach these great truths to trustworthy men who will, in turn, pass them on to others.

"_Judy_, take your share of suffering as a good soldier of Jesus Christ, just as I do, and as Christ's soldier do not let yourself become tied up in worldly affairs, for then you cannot satisfy the one who has enlisted you in His army.

"And _Mark_, follow the Lord's rules for doing His work, just as an athlete either follows the rules or is disqualified and wins no prize.

"_Kathy_, work hard like a farmer who gets paid well if he raises a large crop.

"Let everyone here tonight think over these three illustrations, and may the Lord help you all to understand how they apply to you.

"_Donny_, don't forget the wonderful fact that Jesus Christ was a Man born into King David's family; and that he was God, as shown by the fact that He rose again from the dead. It is because I, Paul, have preached these great truths that I am in trouble here and have been put in jail like a criminal. But the Word of God is not chained, even though I am.

"And _Tommy_, you too should be like the Apostle Paul, more than willing to suffer if that will bring salvation and eternal glory in Christ Jesus to those God has chosen.

"_Karen_, be comforted by this truth, that when you suffer and die for Christ it only means that you will begin living with Him in heaven.

"And if you think that your present service for Him is hard, _Mike_, just remember that someday you are going to sit with Him and rule with Him. But if you give up when you suffer, and turn against Christ, then He must turn against you.

"Even when you are too weak to have any faith left _Nate_, He remains faithful to you and will help you, for He cannot disown you who is part of Himself, and He will always carry out His promise to you.

"_Jenny_, remind your friends of these great facts, and command them in the name of the Lord not to argue over unimportant things. Such arguments are confusing and useless, and even harmful.

"Work hard _Ginger_, so God can say to you, 'Well done!' Be a good workman, one who does not need to be ashamed when God examines your work. Know what His Words say and mean.

"_Jim_, steer clear of foolish discussions which lead people into the sin of anger with each other. Things will be said that will burn and hurt for a long time to come. Hymenaeus and Philetus, in their love of argument, are men like that. They have left the path of truth, preaching the lie that the resurrection of the dead has already occurred; and they have weakened the faith of some who believe them.

"But _Darrell_, God's truth stands firm like a great rock, and nothing can shake it. It is a foundation stone with these words written on it for you _Marci_, 'The Lord knows those who are really His,' and 'A person who calls himself a Christian should not be doing things that are wrong.'"

The above consisted only of II Timothy 2:1-18. If more students are involved, II Timothy chapters 2 through 4 and I Timothy 4:7-5:2 lend themselves well for personal adaptation. (Contributed by Timothy Quill, Appleton, Wisconsin)

WHAT? ME WORRY?

Worry is something we all do. The following is a stimulating outline for a discussion on "worry."

1. Respond to these statements:
   a. Christians should never worry.
   b. Why worry?
   c. If you don't care enough to worry, you don't care.

2. List some things that you worry about.

3. List some things that your parents worry about.

4. Can you list any good consequences of worrying?

5. Can you list any bad consequences of worrying?

6. What would you say to someone who was worred about:
   a. Their parents getting a divorce.
   b. Failing in school.
   c. Unconfessed sin.
   d. The recent loss of a boy(girl) friend.
   e. Future plans.
   f. Bad case of acne.
   g. Meaningless prayer life.
   h. A recent failure.
   i. Death.
   j. Pregnant and unmarried.

THE WINDOW

Read or tell the following story to the group:

The Window

There were once two men, Mr. Wilson and Mr. Thompson, both seriously ill in the same room of a great   hospital. Quite a small room, just large enough for the pair of them. Two beds, two bedside lockers, a door opening on the hall, and one window looking out on the world.

Mr. Wilson as part of his treatment was allowed to sit up in bed for an hour in the afternoon (something to do with draining the fluid from his lungs). His bed was next to the window. But Mr. Thompson had to spend all of his time flat on his back. Both of them had to be kept quiet and still, which was the reason they were in the small room by themselves. They were grateful for the peace and privacy, though. None of the bustle and clatter and prying eyes of the general ward for them. Of course, one of the disadvantages of their condition was that they weren't allowed to do much: no reading, no radio, certainly no television. They just had to keep quiet and still, just the two of them.

Well, they used to talk for hours and hours. About their wives, their children, their homes, their jobs, their hobbies, their childhood, what they did during the war, where they'd been on vacations, all that sort of thing. Every afternoon, when Mr. Wilson, the man by the window, was propped up for his hour, he would pass the time by describing what he could see outside. And Mr. Thompson began to live for those hours.

The window apparently overlooked a park with a lake where there were ducks and swans, children throwing them bread and sailing model boats, and young lovers walking hand in hand beneath the trees. And there were flowers and stretches of grass, games of softball, people taking their ease in the sunshine, and right at the back, behind the fringe of trees, there was a fine view of the city skyline. Mr. Thompson would listen to all of this, enjoying every minute. How a child nearly fell into the lake, how beautiful the girls were in their summer dresses, then an exciting ball game, or a boy playing with his puppy. It got to the place that he could almost see what was happening outside.

Then one fine afternoon when there was some sort of a parade, the thought struck him: Why should Wilson, next to the window, have all the pleasure of seeing what was going on? Why shouldn't *he* get the chance? He felt ashamed and tried not to think like that, but the more he tried, the worse he wanted a change. He would do anything! In a few days, he had turned sour. *He* should be by the window. He brooded. He couldn't sleep and grew even more seriously ill which the doctors just couldn't understand.

One night as he stared at the ceiling, Mr. Wilson suddenly woke up, coughing and choking, the fluid congesting in his lungs, his hands groping for the call button that would bring the night nurse running. But Mr. Thompson watched without moving. The coughing racked the darkness. On and on. He choked and then stopped. The sound of breathing stopped. Mr. Thompson continued to stare at the ceiling.

In the morning, the day nurse came in with water for their baths and found Mr. Wilson dead. They took his body away quietly with no fuss.

As soon as it seemed decent, Mr. Thompson asked if he could be moved to the bed next to the window. So they moved him, tucked him in, made him quite comfortable, and left him alone to be quiet and still. The minute they'd gone, he propped himself up on one elbow, painfully and laboriously, and strained as he looked out the window.

It faced a blank wall.

This beautiful story is not only an excellent illustration for a talk (on a variety of subjects) with its surprise twist at the end, but lends itself well for good discussion possibilities. The following questions raise some of the issues, but are only suggestions and do not have to be followed in any order, nor do all the questions have to be covered. Feel free to develop your own.

1. What was your initial reaction to the story? Were you shocked? Surprised? Angry?
2. From the story, describe Mr. Wilson. What kind of man does he appear to be? Do you like or dislike him? Why?
3. Describe Mr. Thompson. What kind of person is he? Do you like or dislike him?
4. Why did Mr. Wilson do what he did? What do you think his motives were?
5. Would you describe Mr. Wilson's "descriptions" of what was outside the window as: (a) lying? (b) creative imagination? (c) unselfish concern for Mr. Thompson? (d) cruel and envy producing? (e) _____.
6. Did Mr. Wilson do anything wrong?
7. Why did Mr. Thompson's mood change from enjoyment and appreciation to resentment? Was his resentment justified?
8. Did Mr. Thompson *murder* Mr. Wilson?
9. Who was guilty of the more serious wrong? Mr. Wilson or Mr. Thompson?
10. Who was most responsible for Mr. Wilson's death? Why?
11. Would both men have been better off without Mr. Wilson's descriptions of the view outside the window?
12. If you had been Mr. Thompson, how would you have felt when you finally looked out the window and saw nothing but a blank wall? (a) disappointed? (b) angry? (c) guilty? (d) grieved? (e) grateful? (f) puzzled? (g) shocked?
13. Is it a sin to fantasize?
14. Is it a sin to hide the truth or to exaggerate when it doesn't hurt anyone?
15. Where does one draw the line in the areas of fantasy and imagination?

WORSHIP DIARY

This is an idea designed to enrich your group's worship experience and at the same time receive some constructive feedback on this most important area in the church's life. Have each member in your group begin a worship diary in which they write their response to the worship service. They should be writing their responses to questions like, How did I feel? Was I bored? Happy? Moved? What was the response of the people around me? What was most helpful? Least helpful? Did I learn anything? If so, what? Did I feel restricted or inhibited? Did the sermon help me at all? Have the group keep the diary for about four weeks and then have a meeting where everyone compares notes. The discussion following could be quite enlightening. (Contributed by Vernon Edington, Marietta, Ga)

WORKERS IN THE CHURCH

This is a good small group activity which is good for helping people build positive relationships with each other. It also helps people to see how different they all are, yet how important they are to the whole body of Christ. Give each person a list similar to the one below, and have him write in the names of the people in his group beside each "job." After doing so, discussion may follow with each person telling why they made their choices.

1. *The Church Carpenter:* A person who knows how to build relationships with others that are solid, secure, and long lasting.
2. *The Church Electrician:* Someone who adds that extra "spark" to the life of the church.
3. *The Church Engineer:* Someone with the ability to plan things and to make sure that it is done right.
4. *The Church Baker:* The person who adds just the right amount of yeast to every occasion so that it rises successfully.
5. *The Church Security Guard:* Someone who watches out for the welfare of the church and those in it. A person concerned about the well-being of others.
6. *The Church Seamstress:* Someone who has the ability to sew the little tears back together. Someone who is always able to patch things up.
7. *The Church Custodian:* A person who always seems willing to do the dirty jobs that no one else wants to do. Someone who always makes things look a little better than they were.
8. *The Church Tour Guide:* Someone who seems to have the ability to show others the right way to go.
9. *The Church Attorney:* A person who stands up on behalf of others and pleads their cause. One who is concerned with justice and equity.
10. *The Church Publicity Agent:* Someone so excited about the Christian life that he can't keep quiet about it.
11. *Other (write your own)*

(Contributed by Bill O'Connor, Monrovia, California)

UGLY CARDS

How to handle discipline problems with kids is always a burden that youth workers must bear. One suggestion is the use of the "Ugly Card." When a kid blows it - throws a water balloon during prayer, hits the pastor in the nose with a pea shooter, or whatever - he is presented with the dreaded Ugly Card. The Ugly Card is sort of like a traffic ticket, and you can determine for yourself just how bad the penalty will be for getting one. For example, a "first offense" Ugly Card can be like a warning with no significant consequences. However, a second or third might require more severe penalties. Too many Ugly Cards and a person could be sent home (if used at a camp, for example), or must do a specified amount of hard labor (scrubbing floors, washing dishes, windows, etc.) or whatever. The advantage to the Ugly Card system is that the system is spelled out ahead of time for everyone, so that they know the consequences of their actions. But the Ugly Card is at the same time kind of a fun thing, that tends to take the negative edge off of discipline.

An alternative to severe punishment (sending a kid home, banning him from the meetings, hanging him by the thumbs, etc) is to establish a room where kids have to go when they get a certain number of Ugly Cards. This room would have an adult supervisor, but would be separated from the rest of the group. The room could be called the "Time Out Room," the "Love Room," or perhaps the "Nursery." Books, magazines, punching bags, etc. could be available, but no contact with the other kids. The number of Ugly Cards would determine the length of time in this room. (Contributed by Grady Roe, Austin, Texas)

YOUTH GROUP DEVOTIONAL

Instead of using daily devotional guides published by your denomination, have your youth group write their own. This gives the

```
TUESDAY

Ephesians 6:2

    "Honor thy father and mother."

Even though parent-child relationships are not always
the best, each one of us owe a lot to our mothers and
fathers.  From the time we were born, our parents have
loved and cared for us.  My parents have done a lot for
me and they are both very special.  Often though, I
take them for granted and I don't take time to tell
them I love them.

I could do many small things to show them I care.
What keeps me from showing them that I need and
cherish them?  I really don't know.  I do know that
I love them, need them, owe a lot to them, and should
not take them for granted.  To honor my parents would
mean simply to love and respect them.  Today and every-
day, I want to show them just how special they are to
me and how much I care.

                        --Anita Cassis

THOUGHT:  For a few minutes think about all your
          parents have done for you, given you,
          and cared for you.  Today show them
          how special they are to you.  Show
          them love, and thank God if they are
          still alive, that you have this day
          to live with them.
```

```
                                        WEDNESDAY

Matthew 7:1-2

    "Don't criticize, and you won't be criticized.
    For others will treat you as you treat them."

This is another one of those verses that I feel everyone
should follow.  Before I read this verse, I never realized
that one reason people use to criticize me so much was be-
cause I criticized them!  And I did.  I found myself
telling people they had bad tempers, etc., but it never
even crossed my mind to think I had a bad temper!.  So
next time you go to criticize someone, stop and think,
are you really perfect enough to criticize another person?

                        --Kim Francis

THOUGHT:  We really need one another as we walk
          in our everyday life.  We can add so
          much to one another as we share our
          love and importance with each other.
          Today, tell someone in person, and on
          the phone, how much you need them, and
          how thankful you are that they are part
          of your world.
```

young people a chance to express their ideas about the Christian faith. Most importantly, the kids will want to read the devotionals because they know the authors and they can relate to their own peers better. Of course, you could follow any format you want. The one below is from the sample sent to *Ideas*:

(Contributed by Mike Slater, Temple City, California)

YOUTH GROUP REUNION

Here is an idea to encourage better adult-youth communication, and also to give your youth group a sense of its own extended history. Have a reunion of past members of your youth group which can be a party put on by the current group. Go back into the files (if there are any) and invite all those who live near (or far). If the group has a history of being large, then you might want to have a ten year reunion every year and only invite those people who made up the group ten years ago. The kids could research the year (i.e. 1966) and decorate accordingly. The most effective "program" (besides games, refreshments, etc.) would be to allow the invited guests to share some of their memories of the youth group when they were active in it. What did it mean to them? What were some of the things they did? What was their most embarrassing moment? How did the group blow it? Many other questions could be asked as well. This is a great way to get into a group's past and to see its relevance to the group's future. (Contributed by Phil Kennemer, Austin, Texas)

Chapter Four

Special Events

ACTION SCAVENGER HUNT

Here is another creative variation of a scavenger hunt. Each person (or team) receives a list similar to the one below and goes door-to-door as in a normal scavenger hunt. At each house the person at the door is asked to perform one of the actions on the list. If they comply, that item can be crossed off. The team with the most crossed off at the end of the time limit, or the first team to complete the entire list, is the winner. Only one item may be done at each house.

1. Sing two verses of "Old MacDonald."
2. Do 10 jumping jacks.
3. Recite John 3:16.
4. Name 5 movies currently playing local theatres.
5. Yodel something.
6. Run around your house.
7. Start your car's engine and honk the horn.
8. Take our picture.
9. Whistle "Yankee Doodle" all the way through.
10. Say the Pledge of Allegiance.
11. Give us a guided tour of your back yard.
12. Autograph the bottom of our feet.
13. Say "bad blood" ten times very fast.
14. Burp.
15. Do a somersault.

(Adapted from an idea contributed by Larry Maland, Kirkland, Washington)

AIRPORT SCAVENGER HUNT

If you have a major airport in your area you might find this a lot of fun. You also may find out, however, that the airport officials won't consider your game quite so fun. Neither will many of the passengers at the airport. So be sure to brief your kids ahead of time, *not* to be obnoxious, *not* to bother those who don't want to be bothered, *not* to run. After you have done all that, then divide into teams, give them a time limit and have everyone meet back at a pre-determined location at the end of the time limit.

Give them the list below, (you can probably think of other list possibilities as well) and start them all at the same time. It might be wise

to separate the teams into different terminals so that the same people are not being bothered.

1. Find a business man with IBM. (Have him sign name and position)
2. Get a stewardess and have her sign her name.
2. Ask a Krishna person what the greatest value in life is. Write down their response.
4. Find an airline pilot who is going to Hawaii today — name and airline.
5. Find either a couple going on a honeymoon trip or a couple going on a business trip.
6. Find a policeman that is either bald or named Harry.
7. Find out what a first class round trip ticket to Hawaii costs.
8. Find someone with a pilot's license (other than an airline pilot).
9. Find someone who's going back to school on a plane. (Get name of person and school)
10. Ask the lady at the information booth the question she gets asked the most.
11. How many tires does a 747 have?
12. What does VRF stand for and what is it used for?
13. Find a marine on leave from boot camp and ask him in one sentence to describe his "D.I."
14. Find a sailor who's never been on the ocean.
15. Find a maintenance man.
16. Get a shoe shine, have the man sign here (be sure and pay him).
17. Find someone who is in a hurry and offer to help them carry their bags to the gate.
18. Count all the cabs in front of the terminal, get one cabbie to sign.
19. Get a Hertz girl to give you a rental agreement envelope with O.J. Simpson's name on it.
20. How much does a hot dog cost at the snack shop?

(Contributed by Dave Anderson, Burnsville, Minnesota)

ALL PURPOSE PARTY

There are several holidays that occur around the end of the year, and with this "all purpose party," you can celebrate them all at the same time. You can call it a "Halloween - Thanksgiving - Christmas - New Year's Eve - Party" if you prefer, and divide the evening up into four segments. Each segment can be 30 to 45 minutes of celebration of each of the four holidays. Begin with a Halloween party, complete with costumes, Halloween games, cider and doughnuts, ghost stories, etc. Then move to another room which can be decorated for Thanksgiving, and serve turkey with all the trimmings. Then move to a Christmas party with a gift exchange, a visit from Santa, Christmas carols, and so on. Wrap up with a New Year's party, and have clocks appropriately set so that midnight comes when you want it. Have plenty of noisemakers, and a rousing chorus of "Auld Lang Syne." This takes care of all four holidays at once, and can be done anytime in November or December. (Contributed by Ralph Snyder, Akron, Ohio)

BANANA NIGHT II

Here are some more games and activities to include with the others suggested for "Banana Night" in *Ideas Number Sixteen,* page 44.

PASS THE BANANA: Each team sits in a circle with their feet toward the center. At the signal, a banana is passed from person to person cradling the banana with their feet. If the banana is dropped, the person who dropped it becomes the beginning of a new circle so the banana must be passed completely around again. Each team is timed (starting over, of course, if the banana is dropped) and the team with the shortest time wins.

DOCTOR THE BANANA: Each team is given a banana, a knife, and several toothpicks. Within an agreed time limit, each team performs "open banana" surgery. This is done by carefully peeling the banana and slicing it into four equal pieces. These pieces are shown to the judge to verify the cuttings. Then the patients are "cured." This is done by putting the banana back together again, peel and all, using toothpicks where necessary. The winning team is the one with the most "cured" banana.

COUPLES BANANA EAT: Each team selects a couple to represent them. Place a peeled banana with one end in the boy's mouth and the other in the girl's. The first couple to eat the banana without using their hands, wins.

BOBBING FOR BANANAS: Bananas float, so throw a bunch of bananas in a tub of water and "bob for bananas." (Contributed by Pat Caldwell, Tupelo, Mississippi)

BIBLICAL ICE CREAM FESTIVAL

This fund raising project can be a lot of fun for your youth group as well as profitable. In order to make any money, however, you should get the ice cream donated or sold to you at a discount. Serve coffee and punch free with the ice cream creations. Below is a sample listing of ice cream dishes that can be served. Your group can probably come up with more.

THE SEA OF GALILEE
A two scoop vanilla island whose shores are washed by a blue-tinted Seven-up ocean.

THE SUNDAY SUNDAE
One scoop of strawberry ice cream surrounded by six teaspoon sized scoops of vanilla ice cream.

PONTIUS PIE
Take command of the situation by ordering a slice of "Pontius Pie": an ice cream and graham cracker spectacular, distinctly Roman.

THE RED SEA SPLIT
A vanilla ice cream trough filled with homemade strawberry topping for those who desire freedom from the slavery of hunger.

SAMSON AND DELILAH
A sensuous scoop of vanilla covered with a seductive topping sharing the dish with a Samson-sized scoop of chocolate ice cream covered with a full head of chocolate chip "hair."

JOSEPH'S CONE OF MANY COLORS
A cone of rainbow sherbet to refresh you on your way to Egypt (or anywhere else).

THE GARDEN OF EATEN
A well coordinated blend of fruity ice cream and toppings, complete with a snake to tempt you to have another.

SHADRACH, MESHACH, AND ABEDNEGO
Three princely kinds of ice cream surrounded by a fiery furnace of red-hots.

JOHN THE BAPTIST
A unique blend of ice cream, honey and locust-shaped almonds to create a most magnificent creation.

TOWER OF BABEL
A towering combination of assorted ice creams, covered with a variety of toppings, whipped cream, and nuts.

PALM SUNDAE
Two scoops of vanilla ice cream, covered with coconuts and enhanced with a decorative palm frond.

Each of the selections should be printed on a menu with prices listed. The young people create the ice cream spectaculars, wait on the tables, and then after the event is over, have a great party with the ice cream that is left over. Hold it in a good location, advertise it well, and have fun. (Contributed by David Baumann, Garden Grove, California)

BOOK BLAST

Have the youth group write a book. Really tap the creative potential of the group and have the kids write stories, poetry, articles and essays or submit cartoons, drawings, and anything else that can be reproduced. Then have it all edited by a committee, pasted up and printed by the "offset" process. (Photos can be included this way.) A local printer or bindery can bind them into books. Select a catchy title and design a nice cover which can be printed or silk-screened on cover stock. The books can then be advertised and sold in the church and community as a fine fund raising project. (Contributed by Mary McKemy, Lincoln, Nebraska)

BUDGET PROGRESSIVE DINNER

Divide the large group into smaller groups of four people each. (Each should have access to a car and some kitchen space.) Now give each group $7.50 to $10.00 (depending on your budget and size of group) and have them all bring back some part of the meal —appetizer, drink, main dish, fruit, salad, desert, etc. It is important that the groups do not confer with one another which will make for an interesting dinner while at the same time promoting creativity and an exercise in group dynamics. (Contributed by Bruce Coriell, Wheaton, Illinois)

DINNER ON THE GROUP

Here's an idea that has been used successfully to encourage inter-action between old-timers in the group and newcomers who often feel left out. Each week, kids contribute 25 cents to a special "hospitality fund" (or whatever you choose to call it) so that a balance of approximately $30 or so is maintained. Regular members of the group sign up on a list, and each week one person on the list (or perhaps two) are given the hospitality fund to take the newcomers or visitors that week out to dinner. With the money, they pay for the meals and then bring back the unused portion. They may go to a restaurant or may use the money to prepare a dinner at home if they prefer. They can set up the meal for any time during the week that is convenient for everybody.

During the meal, the kids are encouraged to get to know the new-comers, and to invite them to participate in the other activities of the group. This helps new kids to feel more at home and welcome as a part of the youth group rather than as an unwanted intruder. (Contributed by Robert Garris, Windsor, Missouri)

DO YOUR OWN DONUT

This idea breaks the cookie and Kool Aid refreshment routine and is a fun activity as well. Start with several tubes of refrigerated baking powder biscuits available at any supermarket. Form the biscuits into doughnut shapes and drop them into a skillet filled with one inch of cooking oil heated to 375 degrees. Turn when needed and remove when golden brown.

Have a variety of toppings on hand. Chocolate, vanilla, and peanut butter frostings work well. Sprinkles, coconut, and powdered sugar can be added on top of the frosting base. The secret is to let every person make his or her own doughnut creation from the ingredients on hand. Serve with hot chocolate in the winter for a pleasant way to warm up after an outdoor event. Be sure to have plenty of biscuit dough on hand because the doughnuts go fast. Approximately 10 doughnuts can be made from one tube of dough. (Contributed by Craig Johnson, Wheaton, Illinois)

FOTO-MAP

Here's a great variation of the old "treasure hunt" which is not only different, but lots of fun. It works just like the normal treasure hunt - that is, the players all leave at the same time, and go from clue to clue (location to location) in search of the "treasure." The group that gets to the treasure first wins.

"Foto-map" is played similarly, except that the "clues" are photographs. At the starting place, each group or team receives a photograph. The photo is a picture of the first clue location and the group must identify that location by looking at the picture. Obviously, you can make these photos either easy to recognize or almost impossible to recognize. Each group should be traveling by car (or bikes, etc.) and they might have to just drive around until they spot something that looks like their picture. When they figure it out, they go to the location pictured and there they are given the next photo. A good game can consist of anywhere from five to ten clue locations, depending on their difficulty. The group that arrives at the final destination first is the winner. You might give each group a sealed envelope revealing the final destination in case they haven't reached it before a specified time. Before that time, each group must turn in that sealed envelope in order to win. (Contributed by David L. McClary, Tulsa, Oklahoma)

FRISBEE FROLICK

For this special event, all you need is an open field and a few "Frisbees" (available everywhere). Divide the group into teams and play the following Frisbee games:

1. *Distance Frisbee:* Line teams up in columns behind a line and each player gets three throws for distance. After each person throws the Frisbee, a judge marks the spot. The thrower retrieves the Frisbee for the next person in line. Farthest throw and the first team to finish (best combined total) wins.

2. *Accuracy Frisbee:* The teams stay lined up in their columns behind the line and a tire is set upright about 25 feet away from each team. One by one, the team members try to toss the Frisbee through the tire. Again, they retrieve their own Frisbee and return it to the next person in line. The most successful throw wins. Or, each person continues throwing until successful, and the first team to finish wins.

3. *Team Toss Frisbee:* Line up two teams opposite each other about twenty feet apart. The first person on one team throws to

the first person on the other team who tosses the Frisbee back to the second person on the first team, who throws it back to the second person on the second team, and so on. (See diagram.) The thrower's team scores a point if the catcher drops the Frisbee and the catcher's team scores a point if the thrower tosses the Frisbee beyond the reach of the catcher who must keep his feet planted. There should be a neutral judge for each game. You can play to a certain score or until every-everyone has thrown the Frisbee four or five times.

Team One ● ● ● ● ● ● ● ● ● ● ● ● ● ● ● ● ● ●

|/|/|/| etc.

Team Two ● ● ● ● ● ● ● ● ● ● ● ● ● ● ● ● ● ●

4. *Crazy Legs Frisbee:* The teams line up in columns behind a starting line and there is a finish line 20 feet away. Each team has one Frisbee. The first person places the Frisbee between his legs (knees) and runs to the finish line where he tosses the Frisbee back to the next person. If the Frisbee is not caught, the thrower must go back and do the whole routine all over again. First team with all its members across the finish line wins.

5. *Frisbee Water Brigade:* Teams are lined up in columns behind a starting line; each team has a Frisbee (should be the same size for each team), and large pan of water by the starting line, and a wide mouth quart jar about 20 feet away. The object is to get as much water in the jar as quickly as possible by carrying it in the Frisbee. The team that fills the jar the most times in two minutes wins. Obstacles such as chairs to cross, or stairways, etc. add to the fun.

6. *Frisbee Stand-Off:* You need one expendable Frisbee for this one. The object is to get as many people as possible with their feet partially or wholly on the Frisbee or with their weight completely supported by people on the Frisbee. Give them two minutes to practice, and then a one minute period to get the people on. At the end of the time limit, count them. The team with the most on wins.

7. *Freestyle Frisbee:* This is for the "hot dogs." You can have one or two participants from each team demonstrate their best "free-style" Frisbee throw. This could be around the back, under the leg, over the head, double skip, boomerang, or any other kind of fancy or crazy shot. A panel of distinguished and expert judges determine the winners.

There are also other Frisbee games in *Ideas* such as "Fris Ball (Softball played with a Frisbee), "Frisbee Golf," and the "Frisbee

Relay." Check the *Ideaindex* for location and more details. (Contributed by Jim Berkley and Dave Strople, Ventura, California)

HERITAGE DINNER

In order to help kids to get in touch with their own backgrounds and to facilitate communication of this to the other members of the group to get an idea of where each is "coming from," try this variation of the old potluck dinner. Each person is instructed to bring to the event a dish that represents his or her ancestry. Nearly every American has roots in some other nationality, and this could be preceded by a little research into family trees, etc. If a person has many nationalities in his or her background, then one could be chosen. If a person doesn't know of any representative food for his or her ancestry, then more research may be needed.

In addition to the meal, the kids should bring with them a "family treasure" or some relic, photo, or other item of interest that has been passed down through several generations, and be prepared to tell its story. The item need not be valuable except in terms of the story behind it. Another possibility would be to have kids bring baby pictures of themselves that could be posted and have a contest to see who can guess the identity of each picture.

A further extension of this idea would be to have each kid bring or tell about an item that he or she hopes will be passed on to future generations and remembered. You might have each person think of himself as his own grandchild and then talk about "My grandfather...." What kind of a heritage do you hope to leave for your future family? Good discussion and sharing can follow. (Contributed by Jay McKenzie, Moorestown, New Jersey)

HOBBY SHOPS

Here's an idea for getting large groups of junior or senior highs into small groups. Have them vote on a list of hobbies they'd like to learn more about. Take the top 5 or 6 and have everyone choose a group. Find interested adults in your church who will help out one evening a week for six weeks. Generally the most effective leaders are those who are not professionals, but are fairly expert in their hobby field. Possibilities are endless: cooking (boys love this), drama, auto repair, chess, model building, gymnastics (borrow equipment from the "Y" or a local school), crafts (macrame, tie-dying, etc.), photography. The kids will come up with their own ideas.

On the seventh week, have an Appreciation Dinner. Invite all your teachers and their spouses, your minister, and anyone else who might be interested. Each Hobby Shop group shows what it's been up to. The cooking group could make part of the meal. The drama group performs a one-act play; the chess group might demonstrate a few power plays on a gigantic board. Use your imagination. Kids learn something new and beome close friends with those in their group. (Contributed by Barbara Nelson, Royal Oak, Michigan)

JOGGING CLUB

Start a "jogging club" that gets together two or three times a week in the morning to run. There are lots of people who would enjoy this, but need the proper motivation. Use a track field, or somewhere that traffic, dogs, etc. are not a problem. This can be a great way to build relationships with certain kids, plus the obvious physical and health benefits. (Contributed by Bill Rudge, High Point, North Carolina)

LATE GREAT SKATE

Here's one way to put new life into the old roller skating party that used to be so popular. First of all, make arrangements to rent a roller rink for your own private use. Usually you can get one for a flat rate plus skate rentals. Also, make sure you have the freedom to plan your own skating program, rather than being confined to the normal "all skate, couples only, grand march," ad nauseum, kind of thing. You might want to consider an "all night" skate that starts around midnight and goes until dawn. Roller rinks are easier to get at such a ridiculous hour.

The basic idea is to play all sorts of games on skates. Many of the games in the *Ideas* series can be played on skates, giving them an added dimension of fun. Races, relays, ball games, all can be done on skates. Just be sure that the games are not too rough, to avoid possible injuries.

Some sample roller skating games:

1. *Rag Tag:* Everyone gets a rag that hangs out of their back pockets or hangs out of their pants. On a signal, everyone starts skating in the same direction. The object is to grab someone else's rag without having yours taken by another skater. Once your rag is gone, you are out of the race. Awards are given for most rags grabbed by one person, and for whoever stayed in the longest.

2. *Obstacle Course Relay:* Set up an obstacle course which the skaters must skate through. The first team to have each of its members skate through it (one at a time, is the winner.

3. *Triple Skate:* Have everyone skate around the rink in threes. No

passing is allowed. On a signal, the skater in the middle, or on the right or left, moves up to the next threesome. This is good as a mixer.

4. *Scooter Race:* Have one kid down on his haunches who is pushed by another skater. Set a number of laps for the race.

5. *Tumbleweed:* Have all the skaters go down to a squat when the music stops or when the whistle blows. This will tire them quickly.

6. *One-legged Race:* Skaters race, skating with only one skate on. The other foot is used to push.

7. *Run the Gauntlet:* Girls line up in two parallel lines and the boys skate between them with balloons tied to their seats. The girls try to pop the balloons with rolled up newspapers as they skate by. Another way to do this would be to have clothespins (3) fastened to each boy's back, and the girls try to grab the clothespins as the boys skate by. Awards are given to the girl who grabs the most clothespins, and to the boy who lasted the longest.

8. *London Bridge:* Two skaters stand opposite each other, grab hands and form a "bridge" that other skaters can skate under. Each team then lines up and on a signal, begins skating under the bridge. Once under the bridge, each skater circles around and goes through again, as many times as possible before the time limit is up. There should be a counter standing by the bridge, counting the skaters as they pass under the bridge. The team that gets the most skaters under the bridge in the time limit wins.

There are many other possibilities, of course. For breathers, you might want to show some films, serve sandwiches and refreshments, or whatever else you can get away with. (Contributed by Ron Richey, Louisville, Kentucky)

NEW FASHIONED BOX SOCIAL

This is just like the old fashioned box social except that in this case the *boys* pack the box lunches for two and the girls bid for them. With the right encouragement, some guys will go all out and bring fancy dishes, table cloth, candles, soft music, and so on. The girls can bring canned food (later to be given to a needy organization or family) and bid on the lunches using the cans as money. The cans are worth the prices marked on them. (Contributed by Jim Berkley, Ventura, California)

PHONE BOOK BIKE RALLY

For this event, each kid is instructed to bring a phone book and a bike. Kids may also need back-packs or baskets to carry the phone books while riding. A list of locations is passed out to everyone (on separate slips, so that each person will take them in a different order) and each kid must obtain the information asked for. No phone calls are allowed. Each location must be visited. The following list is a sample. You obviously will need to select places in your own city that can be looked up in a phone book. The first person to complete their list within the time limit is the winner. This can also be done in cars.

1. Ed Saldin's Drug Store: *What hours are posted on the front door?*
2. Yo Yo's Cafe: *What number telephone pole is directly behind the building?*
3. Loving Day Care Center: *What kind of animals are on either side of the front door?*
4. San Marco Apartments: *What product is advertised on their sign?*
5. Guthrie Cabinet and Millwork Shop: *How many panes of glass above the sign on the front of the building?*
6. Spratt's Metal Works: *What does the traffic sign directly in front of the building say?*
7. Anderson's Grocery: *What kind of flour is stacked in the front window?*
8. Yakima Ambulance and Towing: *How many trees growing in front of the building?*
9. Hobbit Shoppe Antiques: *Name the farm implement hanging over the front door.*
10. Apple Tree Gift Shop: *The display in the front window features glassware and what?*
11. The Walter J. Farnsworthy home: *What kind of flowers in the front yard?*

(Contributed by Sonny Salsbury, Yakima, Washington)

PIZZA HUNT

This event is good if you live in a city where there are lots of pizza restaurants. Divide into teams that can travel together by car. Everyone leaves at the same time, and the object is to go to as ·many pizza places as possible (within a given time limit) and eat one pizza at each stop. Every time a group arrives at a location, they go inside, order a pizza, wait for it, pay for it, and then eat it together before leaving for the next place. This game teaches not only patience and where to find the best pizza in town, but also the value of phoning in your order ahead of time. (Contributed by Tom Salmon, Snohomish, Washington)

SUPERSTAR COMPETITION

Here is an activity that is fun to do anytime, but is especially great at camps. It is patterned after ABC-TV's "Superstar" competition, in which participants compete in a variety of events. The best overall score is the winner. Normally, there are ten events (you may have any number you want). Each participant selects seven to compete in. If you prefer, you can make everyone compete in all of them, but by giving the kids their choice of seven, it helps to equalize things a little bit. In TV's version, only the top three contestants in each event score points, but you may want to allow the top ten in each event to receive points. For example, first place would receive 10 points, second place would get 9 points, and so on. If someone were to take first place in all seven of his events (very unlikely), he would get a score of 70 points total.

It is best to choose events that do not give a huge advantage to kids who are athletically inclined,   older, smarter, or whatever. This way everyone has a chance (literally) and the competition is more fun for everyone involved. Some sample events:

1. Water balloon shot put (for distance)
2. Shoe kick (hang shoe loosely on foot and kick it for distance)
3. Rowboat race (or kayaks or paddling with hands in an inner tube for time)
4. Diving (judge for ugliest dive or cannonball, or biggest splash)
5. Baseball hitting (use volleyball or have kids hit wrong-handed)
6. Sack race (in potato sacks)
7. Paper airplane throw (for distance in the air. Make your own airplane)
8. Stilts race (best time)
9. Dart throwing (at dartboard or at balloons)
10. Math quiz (give kid a problem, must solve it in the fastest time)
11. Joke telling contest or dramatic reading contest (judged)

At camp, certain events can be held each day. Otherwise, you can have all the events going simultaneously, and the kids go from event to event and their score is recorded in each one that they enter. After everyone is finished, winners in each event are declared. Whoever has the most points (total) is then declared the "Superstar" and is awarded an appropriate "trophy" (be creative with this). (Adapted from an idea contributed by Ken Lentz, Denver, Colorado)

Chapter Five

Skits

AS THE STOMACH TURNS

Here is an impromptu promotional skit which requires only preparation by the narrator. Select your players and put them in their appropriate places on stage. Instruct the cast to carry out the action suggested by each line of narration read. Read the narration, dramatically and with great pathos. Pause after each line until players have finished the required action.

Players:

Narrator
Lucille Lovelorn (best played by a guy)
Philip Pharpar (holding a picture frame in front of him)
Franklin Pharpar (with ring and phony check)
A door (a person standing using fist as doorknob)
A table (one or two people on their hands and knees)
A telephone (a person sitting on table using arm as receiver)

Props:

A ring
A phony check

The narration:

And now, the _____ present another episode in the continuing life drama, " As the Stomach Turns." Last time, luscious Lucille Lovelorn had spurned Dr. Preakbeak's advances because her precious Philip Pharpar would soon be graduating from Law School and they would be married.

Today's scene opens with Lucille standing next to the picture of Philip which is hanging on the wall of her apartment.
Lucille is humming a happy tune to herself as she stares wistfully at her beloved Philip.
"Philip, I miss you so much," she said as she caressed his cheek.
"Hurry home to me," she begged.
Then, she kissed his picture passionately.
Suddenly, the telephone rang.
Lucille pranced to the table, picked up the receiver and sweetly said, "Hello."
She smiled and said, "Oh, Gladys, it's you."
Then she frowned darkly.
Philip had found someone new. Philip had told Gladys to tell Lucille goodbye forever.

Lucille slammed down the receiver angrily and began to cry.
She ran over to the picture of Philip and screamed, "You cad."
Then she slapped his picture viciously, and began to cry louder.
She took the picture of Philip and turned it to the wall; and began to cry louder.
Then she threw herself on the floor and began to cry louder.
Suddenly, Franklin Pharpar, Philip's younger brother, approached the door and began to knock vigorously.
Lucille got up, straightened her hair and skirt, and jerked open the door.
Franklin entered the room quickly and said, "Lucille, have you been crying?"
"What's it to you, Batface?" pouted Lucille.
Then she slapped him painfully across the face.
Franklin slammed the door as viciously as Lucille had slapped him.
"I'm sorry," cried Lucille.
Then she began to weep upon his shoulder.
"Philip left me," she sobbed as she pointed to the telephone.
"Tommyrot," said Franklin as he stepped back quickly.
"He does love you," he said.
"He sent me with this for you," he said.
Lucille gave a shriek of joy as she took the ring from Franklin's hand.
Then she gave Franklin a big hug.
Lucille leaped to Philip's picture and spun it around to face her.
"I love you too, darling," she cooed.
Then she kissed his picture even more passionately than before.
Lucille began dancing around the room with Franklin.
Suddenly, the telephone rang again.
Lucille hopped to the phone and jerked up the receiver.
"Hello, hello, hello," she sang happily.
"Oh, Philip, it's you," she sighed.
But then a frown clouded her face.
He *had* found someone else; they *were* through.
She slammed down the receiver and angrily threw the ring to the floor.
Then she whirled and slapped Franklin.
"You are a liar," she screamed.
Then she jumped to Philip's picture.
"You are a worthless animal," she shrieked.
Then she slapped his picture mercilessly.
Then she wrenched the picture from the wall, and threw it to the floor.
Franklin dropped to one knee and clasped his hands.
"But I love you, my flower,' he sang.
"And I have something more valuable than a ring for you, my pet," he said.
Then Franklin pulled a check from his pocket for the amount of

_____.
Here was the supreme gift. He wanted to pay her way to
_____.
Lucille squealed with delight.
"What a lovely thought, darling," she sighed.
They embraced happily.
Then they walked over Philip's picture and out the door to their new life ahead.

(Contributed by Ed Stewart, Glendale, California)

THE BERMUDA TRIANGLE

Characters:	Luther Capehart, affable talk show host. Horace Q. Quivermayer, Bermuda Triangle man.
Props:	Two chairs. Maybe a coffee table or a plastic plant.
Script:	
Luther:	Hello and welcome to Put Up Or Shut Up, a talk show where, each week, we try to find something new and interesting to talk about. Of course sometimes that isn't as easy as it sounds, but this week I'm sure we've got a winner. Well, I'm not *sure*, I *hope* we have a winner. *(Quivermayer loudly clears his throat.)*
Luther:	*(suddenly aware he's babbling)* Yes! Well, we shall see, shan't we? My name is Luther Capehart and tonight our guest is Mr. Horace Q. Quivermayer. Mr. Quivermayer will be discussing with us the mysterious and interesting, we hope, secret of the Bermuda Triangle. Welcome Mr. Quivermayer.
Quivermayer:	Thank you.
Luther:	My notes tell me that you are one of the kissing. Just what does that mean?
Quivermayer:	I have no idea.
Luther:	You have no idea?
Quivermayer:	Not an inkling.
Luther:	*(uneasily looking off stage for an explanation)* What? Oh. *(back to Quivermayer)* My aides tell me the notes should read "one of the missing." Must be a typographical error. Are you indeed one of the missing?
Quivermayer:	That I am.
Luther:	Ah-ha. Now we're getting somewhere. Where are you missing from?

Quivermayer:	At the moment everywhere. I am originally missing from Willow Wisp, Missouri.
Luther:	And how did you come to be missing?
Quivermayer:	Do you mean, how did I happen to fall into the mysterious secret of the Bermuda Triangle?
Luther:	Exactly.
Quivermayer:	Well, it all started on our homemade sloop, The Abalone. I was with my wife, my three kids and Bunky, our dog. We were sailing along—
Luther:	You were sailing along—
Quivermayer:	On Moonlight Bay—
Luther:	On Moonlight Bay—
Quivermayer:	We could hear the voices singing—
Luther:	What did they seem to say?
Quivermayer:	I haven't the foggiest. That was the moment we fell into the mysterious secret of the Bermuda Triangle.
Luther:	That's when you disappeared.
Quivermayer:	That was the moment.
Luther:	What was it like?
Quivermayer:	Pardon me?
Luther:	What was it like? Tell us what happened after you fell into the mysterious secret of the Bermuda Triangle.
Quivermayer:	Oh, I couldn't do that.
Luther:	Pardon me?
Quivermayer:	I couldn't tell you about what happened.
Luther:	Why not?
Quivermayer:	It wouldn't be a mysterious secret then, would it?
Luther:	I see. Well, could you tell us about the accommodations without giving away the location?
Quivermayer:	I don't think so.
Luther:	Just a hint?
Quivermayer:	Nope.
Luther:	How about a mailing address in case some of the folks want to get in touch with you?
Quivermayer:	I'm afraid not.
Luther:	A box number?
Quivermayer:	No.
Luther:	In that case, since we seem to have covered as much as we can, Mr. Quivermayer, I'd like to thank you for not being here tonight.
Quivermayer:	My pleasure.

(Contributed by John C. Moyer, Philadelphia, Pa.)

THE BIG DATE

Bill and Karen have just met each other after being introduced by common friends. This is the first date for both. They have just arrived at a local restaurant for a meal.

Bill: (embarrassed) Hi Karen.

Karen: (Equally embarrassed) Hi Bill.

Bill: (Still embarrassed) Hi Karen.

Karen: (Still embarrassed) Hi Bill.

Bill: Gosh, this is so . . . (He leaves sentence floating)

Karen: Yes, it is so . . . (She also leaves the sentence floating)

Bill: Karen, eh, have you had many dates before?

Karen: The only date I've ever had was on August 13th.

Bill: Oh really, what was that?

Karen: My birthday. (Karen then drops her comb on the floor)

Bill: Oh here! I'll get it. (As he stoops over, he falls down on the floor.) I guess I fell for that one, but at least I had a nice trip. (As Bill stands up, he forgets to pick up the comb.)

Karen: Oh, Bill, you're so funny! (suddenly serious) But would you mind picking up my comb?

Bill: (embarrassed) Oh yeah, I guess I forgot. (As Bill squats down, sound effects are heard of his pants ripping. As he reaches behind him to check out that part ripped, he falls backwards from his squatting position over to his back. At that moment a waiter comes to take the order and not seeing Bill, trips over him and falls to the floor.)

Karen: Oh my goodness!

Waiter: (regaining composure) What in the world were you doing on the floor sir? Aren't our seats comfortable enough?

Bill: Oh no. The seats are just fine. I was just checking to see if the floor was on the level.

Waiter: (unbelievingly) I don't know about the floor, but are you on the level? (waiter then notices the rip, and seeing the chance for a pun replies . . .) By the way sir, something terrible has happened to your pants.

Bill: Yes I know. Isn't that a rip-off? (both men stand)

Waiter: Well would you like me to do anything?

Bill:	Yea, how about turning your head when I leave?
Waiter:	(unbelievingly) Sure thing . . . Hey, I'll be back in a minute to take your order. (As waiter leaves, Bill sits back down at the table.)
Karen:	Bill, I really appreciate your efforts, but my comb is still on the floor.
Bill:	I'm sorry, Karen, but that waiter crushed my ear when he fell on me. What did you say?
Karen:	I said my comb is still on the floor.
Bill:	(sheepishly) Your phone is in the store?
Karen:	No! MY COMB IS ON THE FLOOR !
Bill:	(sheepishly) Oh! I'm sorry. (bends down and gets the comb) Well, we may as well order, there's no use in waiting around.
Karen:	I don't mind waiting. Sometimes I even like to wait around.
Bill:	What?
Karen:	I said, it gives me a lift sometimes to wait.
Bill:	Yea. I like weightlifting too.
Karen:	Oh good-grief. Not to change the subject, but what did you do today?
Bill:	I got things all straightened out.
Karen:	What do you mean?
Bill:	I mean I did my ironing. Aren't you *impressed?*
Karen:	Not a great deal. I did my laundry today.
Bill:	I thought I smelled bleach! But I thought it was just your hair.
Karen:	(offended) Well, I never . . .
Bill:	Well you ought to, I can't stand the color of your hair.
Karen:	BILL! You've hurt my feelings!
Bill:	(bashfully) Oh, I'm sorry. Speaking of laundry, do you know the money changing machines they have in there?
Karen:	Well, not personally, but go ahead.
Bill:	Well I wanted to prove how stupid those machines are, so I put a 5 dollar bill in one and it still gave me change for a dollar. Just to make sure it was no fluke, I put a 10 dollar

173

bill in the next time and it *still* gave me change for a dollar. I bet you never realized how *stupid* those machines are, have you?

Karen: That doesn't make sense.

Bill: What do you mean?

Karen: I mean you lost 13 dollars and you are saying the *machines* are stupid.

Bill: Well, I only did it for a change.

Karen: That's what all the money changers are for; a change.

Bill: That makes sense.

Waiter: I don't mean to interrupt, but are you ready to order?

Bill: Huh?

Waiter: Your order?

Bill: What?

Waiter: ORDER, ORDER !

Bill: What are you, a judge?

Waiter: I don't know about that, but whenever I go to play tennis I wind up in a court.

Bill: You ought to get out of that racket.

Waiter: *(looks up and states pleadingly)* Why me? . . . Have you decided what you would like to eat?

Bill: Yes, I'll take the New York Sirloin steak, baked potatoe, corn, tossed salad with French dressing and a large Coke. That's all.

Karen: What about me, Bill?

Bill: *(surprised)* Aren't you going to buy your own?

Karen: Of course not, it's not proper.

Bill: O.K. O.K. Waiter, she'll have a small Coke.

Waiter: You're not going too far *overboard* are you?

Bill: Don't be silly. We're nowhere near water, much less on a ship.

Karen: You may be right there, but you're *still* all wet. *(Karen then throws her glass of water all over Bill and they exit.)*

(Contributed by Bruce Humbert, Wichita Falls, Texas)

CREATIVE THEME SKITS

Here's a fun idea for retreats or youth meetings that is creative and involves total participation. Put several ordinary objects in as many sacks as you have teams. Objects should be things like: paper clip, que-tip, popcicle stick, etc. Put the *same* things in each sack and give each team twenty minutes to form a skit around a selected theme. The skit can be serious or funny but each team must use every item in the sack and every team member must be involved.

After the time limit have each team present their skit. (Contributed by Joe Snow, Midwest City, Oklahoma)

THE GREATEST SHOW ON EARTH

Here is a fun skit that contains a grand total of 56 puns guaranteed to bring 56 groans. The cast:

The Announcer
Boss Leland, Owner of
  the Big Top Circus
Bobo the Clown,
  Leland's assistant
Bill Blade

Electro, the Human Wall
  Socket
Nelson Fury, the Human Bullet
Barney Tomb, the Modern Mummy
Creepy Terry Tiptoe,
  the Tightrope Terror

Announcer:	Boss Leland's Big Top Circus has just arrived in the small country town of Grissle. Boss now attempts to organize his troupe of performers. He calls for his best friend and trusty sidekick, Bobo, the Clown.
Boss:	Bobo, come here, Do you have any idea what Grissle is like?
Bobo:	I hear it's a pretty tough town.
Boss:	Really? I find that awfully hard to swallow. Bobo, this year's circus schedule is very demanding. I'm afraid we're going to have to limit the number of acts we have. Some of the ones we have now will have to go. I wrote up a list of doubtfuls. I want you to get Bill Blade and bring him here. I want to talk to him about his knife act.
Announcer:	So Bobo brings Bill Blade to Boss. *(They enter.)*
Boss:	Well, well, Bill, don't you look sharp today.
Bill:	You wanted to see me, Boss?
Boss:	Yes, I do.
Bill:	It's about my knife act, isn't it?

Boss:	I'm afraid so. Face it, Bill, your knife act just doesn't cut it around here anymore.
Bobo:	Yeah. It always was a bit dull.
Bill:	Oh, I get the point. You don't think I can hack it. Well, I admit I'm a bit rusty, but I still have an edge on the other performers.
Boss:	I'm sorry, Bill, but I've tried to carve you into a competent circus star, but you haven't done well with your job. No matter how you slice it, it's time for you to switch, Blade.
Announcer:	So Bill Blade sadly leaves his circus home. *(He exits, weeping.)*
Bobo:	I think your words pierced his heart.
Announcer:	Boss now calls in his next candidate on the list of doubtfuls, Electro, the Human Wall Socket. *(Enter Electro.)*
Boss:	Electro, I want to talk to you about something.
Electro:	Really? Watt?
Boss:	I have some bad news for you.
Electro:	If it's about last month's electric bill, I can explain . . .
Boss:	No, it's nothing to do with that. This may come as a shock to you, but I'm pulling the plug on your act.
Electro:	But why? I've only been here a few weeks. Couldn't you give me an extension?
Boss:	It's out of the question.
Electro:	You can't get rid of me that way. I've got connections!
Boss:	Now don't blow a fuse. You've traveled the whole circuit with us, but due to the current situation, I've got to disconnect you from the Big Top Circus.
Electro:	But I'm the highlight of the show!
Boss:	Go fly a kite.
Announcer:	So Electro also sadly leaves his circus home. *(He exits.)*
Bobo:	He never was very bright.
Boss:	Who's next on the list?

Bobo:	Nelson Fury, the Human Bullet.
Boss:	He's probably in the powder room. Bring him in. It should be fairly easy to fire the Bullet.
Announcer:	So Bobo, Boss's best buddy, brings Bullet.
Boss:	Hello, Nelson.
Nelson:	Hi Boss. You want to talk to me?
Boss:	Yes, it's about your act.
Nelson:	My act? Has it triggered something in your mind?
Boss:	Not exactly, Nelson. I realize that you are a big shot around here, but I'm letting you go.
Nelson:	But why? My act has always been loaded with excitement. Everyone says it's a barrel of laughs.
Boss:	Be reasonable. Surely a man of your calibre can understand. I've always gotten a big bang out of your act, but you'll have to find a new job somewhere else.
Nelson:	I hate to be such a revolver. Shoot!
Announcer:	And so the Human Bullet leaves the Big Top forever. *(He leaves.)*
Boss:	Well, that's the last we'll see of him.
Bobo:	The old son-of-a-gun.
Announcer:	Suddenly Bobo is handed some dreadful news!
Bobo:	Boss, I've been handed some dreadful news!
Boss:	What is it?
Bobo:	Barney Tomb, the Modern Mummy is quitting our circuit!
Boss:	What? Bring him here. I want my Mummy!
Announcer:	So Bobo brings the Modern Mummy to Boss. *(They enter.)*
Boss:	What's this I hear about you quitting?
Barney:	That's right. I'm getting tired of all this.
Boss:	You're kidding.
Barney:	No, I'm dead serious.
Boss:	You're always so wrapped up in your work. Maybe you need a vacation to unwind a little bit. You'd feel a

	lot better.
Barney:	No, I'm tired of being buried in responsibility. And my health . . . I'm coffin all the time.
Boss:	Where did you dig up that excuse?
Barney:	This is a grave situation, Boss. Don't take it lightly. This circus routine bores me stiff.
Boss:	I can't help it if things have been a little dead lately.
Barney:	Don't try shoveling the blame on someone else, Boss. Good Bye!
Announcer:	And Barney the Modern Mummy angrily stomps out of the circus. *(Exits.)*
Bobo:	His act never was very lively.
Boss:	Who's next on our list?
Bobo:	Creepy Terry, the Tightrope Terror. I'll go get him.
Announcer:	So Creepy Terry, the Tightrope Terror tiptoes in to see the Boss. *(He does.)*
Terry:	Hi Boss. What's up?
Boss:	Terry, I'm afraid your tightrope act is going to take a fall.
Terry:	You're pulling my leg.
Boss:	We're having trouble balancing the budget, and you've been getting out of line lately.
Terry:	That's a lie! I've always been a steady worker. Wire you doing this to me?
Boss:	We're tired of stringing you along.
Terry:	But Boss, I've always walked the line! And don't forget that I've got friends in high places!
Boss:	Sorry, Terry, You're out! We're tired of you acting like you were above us all.
Terry:	I'm a level-headed guy, but you've stretched this too far! I quit!
Announcer:	Creepy Terry tiptoes out of the circus.
Boss:	Well, Bobo, that's the end of our list. In a way it's kinda sad to see them all go.
Bobo:	But Boss, doesn't this play have a happy ending?

Boss: Sure Bobo. Everyone will be happy to know that this play is now over.

(Contributed by Chris Herpolsheimer, La Mesa, California)

KID RINGO

This skit centers around the old west and would be great at a banquet or party where the theme is western. JESSE JONES should be dressed in full cowboy regalia, look mean and wear his guns low. KID RINGO is a very *old man* who is still trying to live by his legend. He should have spurs, big hat, and barely be able to get around.

NARRATOR: In the West of the 1880's violent men dictated the only law of the times. Those who carried the gun were the powerful — imposing their will upon peaceful men and women. The highest law of the land was written on the barrel of a Colt 44. Often, cruel men preyed upon innocents, taking whatever they wanted. But sometimes, men of the gun met each other in battle for prize, possession or reputation. These "Showdowns' were terrible clashes — the poetry of destruction as written by the pen of hate dipped in an inkwell of blood.

JESSE: *(He stops at stage, takes out his gun, checks it carefully by rotating the cylinder, then holsters it again. He frees his shoulder and arm muscles by several stretches and shrugs. He then loosens up his hands and cracks his knuckles. Now satisfied that his is ready, he sets himself with a mean look and a slight crouch, hands ready at his guns. He yells.)*
Kid! Kid Ringo! I'm callin you out! *(no answer) (louder)* KID, I know you're in there. It's me, Jesse Jones. You've eluded me long enough. You're goin to meet me in the street today and the devil in hades tonight, Kid! *(The door slowly opens and Kid Ringo begins to come out onto the stage. He shuffles slowly up.)*

KID: The "devil in hades" huh? You cain't say that in front of all these ladies.

JESSE: *(incredulously)* I cain't! Well I just *did!!*

KID: Well, I guess you've got a point there. *(He turns and begins to leave)*

JESSE: Where you goin?

KID: Back to watch the girls go by in the hotel lobby.

JESSE: Why?

KID: I don't remember.

JESSE: Get back here and prepare to throw hot lead. *(He takes*

179

step or two toward Kid and spurs jingle)

KID: What's that funny noise?

JESSE: Them's ma' spurs. Don't you wear spurs, Kid?

KID: Don't wear em anymore after the wife died.

JESSE: Never mind, Ringo, I've killed 37 men and I'm aimin to make you 38. How many've you killed?

KID: Let's see ... *(begins to count slowly on hands, then drops down to take off one boot, when he starts taking off second boot, Jesse interrupts.)*

JESSE: *(mad)* Nevermind, you old coot, Reach for your guns.

KID: Wait a minute, I'm not warm yet. *(Kid goes through a warm-up procedure like Jesse, except for the gun. When he tries to crack his knuckles, he is unable to do so for lack of strength. Finally he puts his hands under his boots and tries to stand up.)*

JESSE: C'mon Kid, go for your gun.

KID: Not so fast. Let's do it the old way. Back to back, we take 5 paces, turn, draw and fire.

JESSE: I don't care how I kill you, let's just do it. *(They come together at stage center, turn back to back.)*

JESSE: Ready? 1, 2, 3, 4, 5! *(He turns and begins to draw ... but Kid Ringo is still shuffling and beginning to turn around)* You're not even ready you dumb old coot. Just back away. I'll give you a chance. You can draw first. When I count 3 you go for your gun. OK?

KID: OK.

JESSE: One! Two! Three! *(pause)* Well, go for your gun.

KID: I am. *(His hand slowly creeps toward his gun)*

JESSE: This is the last chance I'm givin you, Kid. No more stalling, you'd better be ready, cause this time I'm pullin down on you. Are you loaded?

KID: I wish I were.

JESSE: Nah, I mean the gun, stupid.

KID: Wait a minute, I'll see *(He pulls his gun out and twirls the cylinder. The barrel is pointed away toward the front of stage. As he checks the gun, it goes off. One of the spectators on the front row gasps and slides off the chair, clutching his chest.)*

JESSE: Now you've done it. You've killed an innocent bystander. You're the worst gunfighter I've ever seen. Don't you even know how to use a gun?

KID: I didn't mean to do it ... I was just checking my gun and it went off. It must have a bad trigger or something. *(He's pointing the gun down and towards Jesse, and it fires. Jesse groans and slumps to the floor toward the Kid so that he's almost at his feet. The Kid is unaware that Jesse has been shot.)* Did it again. I'd better fight you before I

180

shoot all my bullets. *(Turns toward where Jesse stood and squints, trying to see him)* Where'd he go? Run off like all them others. *(Holsters gun)* Yup, they all turns to jelly in their boots when they face up to KID RINGO. *(Shuffles offstage.)*

(Contributed by Herb Shipp, Big Spring, Texas)

THE ROLLER SKATER

Characters:	Luther Capehart, affable talk show host. Josiah P. Forbes, roller skate man.
Props:	Two chairs. Maybe a coffee table or a plastic plant. Roller skates.
Script:	
Luther:	Hello and welcome to Put Up Or Shut Up, a talk show where we interview all the top name performers and news makers. *(remembering his guest he almost apologizes to the audience)* And, sometimes, when they're not available we talk to *you* the ordinary citizen. My name is Luther Capehart and tonight we have with us a very ordinary citizen, Mr. Josiah P. Forbes. Mr. Forbes is, at this very moment, in the process of setting the world record for wearing a pair of roller skates.
Forbes:	*(eager)* I sure am!
Luther:	Welcome, Mr. Forbes.
Forbes:	Thank you. It's nice to be here.
Luther:	It's nice having you here.
Forbes:	Well, it's nice being here.
Luther:	*(trying to get down to business)* I think, Mr. Forbes, we should, at the very outset of the show, point out that you are wearing your roller skates not on your feet, as one might imagine, but on your hands.
Forbes:	That's right.
Luther:	Why is that?
Forbes:	Do you mean, why am I wearing these skates on my hands instead of on my feet?
Luther:	Exactly.
Forbes:	I don't know how to skate.
Luther:	But it says here that you are in the process of setting a world record for—
Forbes:	*(interrupting)*—for wearing roller skates. Doesn't say anything about feet, does it?
Luther:	No.
Forbes:	I wouldn't have lasted 87 minutes with these things on

	my feet.
Luther:	(resigned) And how long have you lasted?
Forbes:	87 days.
Luther:	87 days.
Forbes:	87 days.
Luther:	Certainly is a long time.
Forbes:	I want to set a record that will be hard to break. I plan to keep these skates on until Arbor Day.
Luther:	How long will that make it?
Forbes:	I'm not quite sure. Actually, I was hoping you could tell me.
Luther:	Tell you what?
Forbes:	When is Arbor Day?
Luther:	(pauses to think) I'm afraid I don't know. (another pause) Perhaps you could visit your local library.
Forbes:	I tried that.
Luther:	And?
Forbes:	They threw me out. Ever try thumbing through a Britannica with roller skates on your hands? I ripped it up good.
Luther:	I bet you've run into a lot of little problems like that.
Forbes:	I sure have. One thing I found rather difficult was eating mashed potatoes.
Luther:	Keep slipping off your wheels, do they?
Forbes:	They sure do. And another thing is playing pinochle. Do you know how hard it is to shuffle with these things on?
Luther:	(holding up a hand, signaling Forbes to stop) I can imagine. Ha, ha. (The voices of the two now begin to overlap as each man continues his own conversation. Luther, trying to rap the show up. Forbes complaining.)
Forbes:	Or making a phone call? Do you know how hard that is? And try explaining to an operator why you're not dialing direct.
Luther:	That's just fine.
Forbes:	It's near impossible.
Luther:	Well, thank you for joining us tonight, Mr. Forbes. It certainly was a pleasure.
Forbes:	Or playing ping pong?
Luther:	(to audience) That's all for now, folks. Tune in again next time for more of Put Up Or Shut Up.
Forbes:	You can't hold a paddle with a roller skate on your hand.
Luther:	(looking off stage) Are we off? Good.
Forbes:	Just try putting some spin on a ping pong ball while you're wearing a roller skate on your hand. (Luther

182

exits. Forbes follows still complaining.)

Forbes: It can't be done! It just can't be done.

(Contributed by John C. Moyer, Philadelphia, Pa.)

WILL SHE OR WON'T SHE?

Here's a short skit that is good for promoting a coming event that costs money or where dates are encouraged.

Guy: Will she or won't she? Will she or won't she? . . .

Girl: (Walking by) Will she or won't she what?

Guy: Will she or won't she go with me to the _____?

Girl: Who is "she"?

Guy: You.

Girl: Oh, I'd love to!

Guy: Will she or won't she? Will she or won't she? . . .

Girl: What's the matter? I already told you that I'd go with you.

Guy: Will she or won't she buy her own ticket?

Girl: (Slaps guy and chases him off stage. . .)

(Contributed by Roy Bilyen, Shawnee Mission, Kansas)

Chapter Six

Camping

BIBLE PICTURE POSTERS

This can be a creative and stimulating activity for a camp, weekend retreat or all-day outing. Begin with a Bible study and divide into small groups of four or five. Then give each group a Poloroid camera and a roll or two of film. Have the kids go out and shoot a series of pictures that illustrate either the portion of Scripture studied or another of their own choosing. After the pictures are completed, provide poster board, magic markers, tape, etc. and have the groups create posters using their pictures, the Scripture, and their own creativity. The posters are then placed on display and can be enjoyed by everyone. (Contributed by Lavern Kruse, Norfol, Nebraska)

BLIND RETREAT

There are many experiences that help to sensitize young people to the problems of others. This idea is outstanding for that purpose, but requires careful planning and preparation of the participants. Kids at a retreat are blindfolded securely with gauze and bandages for an 18 hour period. During the period, only the sponsors of the group can see, and must help the kids function without their sight. They must eat, sleep, dress, play, and communicate without the use of their eyes for the entire length of time.

The results are astounding. For some kids, the experience is extremely frightening, and they should be allowed to remove the blindfolds if they just can't handle it any longer. But for the kids who stick it out, they are able to understand more fully the plight of the blind and the beauty of sight. Kids do improve as time goes along at getting along without their eyes, but they really learn what it means to be dependent on others.

Follow up the experience with discussion and a study of scripture passages relating to blindness and a worship service thanking God for sight and the beauty of His creation. Note: Be sure that safety precautions are taken to prevent accidents that might occur from kids bumping into things, stumbling or falling.

CAMP CHARIOTS

This is a good idea if you are having a camp that involves a number of youth groups or if you are having team competition and want to generate a little excitement prior to camp. Send a notice to the participating groups asking each to construct a "chariot" that can be brought to camp for the "colossal chariot race" that will be held during camp. The chariot can be constructed out of anything, and should be designed so that four people do the pulling and one person rides. Not only will the chariots be raced, but awards will be given for most imaginative, best design, ugliest, etc. Any size group can bring a chariot to race, and if the group is large, one chariot can be entered for every ten people in the group. This event not only provides a fun activity at camp, but really helps in the promotion of it as well. (Contributed by John Tolle, Modesto, California)

CAMP KIDNAP LETTER

Here's a clever letter idea that can be used both for promotion and as a camp registration and parental permission form. Letters and words are cut from a magazine, pasted down, and printed up in the following manner:

(Contributed by Jim Ulrich, Arlington Heights, Illinois)

FIRING SQUAD

When you announce the camp "rules and regulations," warn the kids that all law breakers will be required to face the "firing squad." The exact details of the "firing squad" don't have to be revealed right away. Sometimes just not knowing just how bad the firing squad is can be a deterrent to camp crime in itself.

When an "execution" is necessary (you can make a big deal out of it and have a mass execution if you have several law breakers), the condemned campers are blindfolded with their hands tied behind their backs. The "firing squad" consists of several of the camp staff who are armed with cans of shaving cream. By replacing the normal nozzle on a can of shaving cream with the sprayer from a can of aerosol spray, the shaving cream shoots out in a long stream with a range of about six feet. "Ready, aim, fire!" (Contributed by Buddy Reed, Maryville, Tennessee)

GET ALONE WITH A TREE

At camp, allow each camper time to select a personal tree (if the camp has enough trees in the area) and "stake it out." They may hang their name on it with a piece of paper and a thumbtack. Each day the kids go to "their tree" at a designated time for personal devotions. This tree remains their tree throughout the duration of the camp for quiet times or meditation. Some mini-messages given by the camp leadership preceding the devotional time can be centered around trees in the Bible (e.g. Zaccheus and the Sycamore tree, The Garden of Eden, The "Tree of Life," The "tree" on which Christ was crucified, etc.). The actual text can then be studied by the campers individually. (Contributed by Frederick H. Schaffner, Salisbury, Maryland)

GREAT CABIN RACE

This is a great camp game that can be used not only for fun competition, but also as a way to get certain chores accomplished and to help kids get to know each other a lot better. Each cabin group works together as a unit with the counselor as the group leader. A "team" consists of several cabins, so long as each team has the same number of cabins.

To start the game, all teams gather at one place. Each team is given a box containing "assignments" written on small pieces of paper. The assignments are kept secret until they are drawn. On a signal, the first cabin on each team draws an assignment and rushes off to complete it as quickly as possible. When that cabin returns, the next cabin draws an assignment, and so on, relay style.

A few sample assignments:

1. Run to your cabin - disrobe - shower - put on sleeping apparel - stay in bed for 3 minutes - arise - make your bed - brush your teeth - get dressed - return to team.

2. Go to your cabin - put on swimsuit - go to pool - wade across the pool four times - return to cabin - get dressed - hang swimsuits on line - back to team.

3. Go to infirmary - sign in - get weighed - get height measured - get reflex test - have pulse rate taken - wash hands - gargle with mouth wash - sign out - return to team.

4. Go to kitchen - make peanut butter and jelly sandwiches - get piece of fruit - put in bag - get sheet - hike to (certain area) - spread out sheet - pick a flower centerpiece - say grace - eat lunch - throw away trash properly - return to team.

5. Other assignments can include washing cars or buses, playing certain games - setting up the dining hall, etc. There is no limit to what you can do.

While each cabin is out doing their assignment, there can be some singing, games, or other activities for the waiting groups. A variation of this would be to give each cabin a list of several assignments, and the first cabin to complete them all is the winner. (Contributed by Norma Bailey, Colora, Maryland)

HAND MADE GIFTS

This is a good idea for camps or weekend retreats. At the beginning of camp, have each kid draw a name from a box containing everyone's name written on a slip of paper. Then ask each person to create a "gift" for the person whose name they drew. The gift should be completed by the end of camp or some other specified time. Materials can be provided such as glue, paints, pieces of wood, metal, string, etc. The gifts can be made of anything, but should be made with that special person in mind. No one should reveal who they are making their gift for until the time when the gifts are exchanged. Follow up with a discussion on giving and receiving, or on the meaning of the various gifts that were created. (Contributed by James Allard, East Canton, Ohio)

MYSTERY MEN

Here's a great way to add a little "mystery" to your next camp or retreat. Select three persons to be "mystery men" (or women) and at each meal, give out clues to their identity. Campers then try to solve the mystery by putting together the clues and asking a lot of questions. The first person to correctly guess the identities of all three wins a prize (or points for his "team," etc.). The three "mystery men" can be people at camp, or famous people (such as Bible characters) that the kids would know. Don't make the clues too easy. Make them tough. As the camp nears its end, the clues can be made easier if no one has been able to guess correctly. (Contributed by Curt Finch, Mclean, Virginia)

RAID REGULATION

Nearly every junior and senior high camp or retreat will include one or more "raids" in which a full-scale water balloon war breaks out in and around the cabins, usually in the middle of the night. Sometimes these raids can get completely out of hand.   One good way to tame them down is to simply plan the notorious "raid" right into the camp schedule, perhaps on a Friday night. On the first day of camp, give each kid a water balloon (or two) attached to a card explaining the rules, boundaries and time limits for the raid. Thus, everyone in the camp is involved which prevents only a few kids having fun at the expense of others. It's also much easier than trying to squelch the inevitable. (Contributed by Luke Harkey, Orlando, Florida)

ROTATE

This is a camp activity, ideal for rainy weather, especially when it has been raining for several days, and there is nothing but mud and wetness all around. It also is good when you don't have a large indoor room to hold games and activities in on rainy days. The campers are divided into small groups of anywhere from 10 to 25 kids each, depending on your situation. Cabins are cleared as much as possible of debris and beds are arranged so that there is room for kids to move around. Campers are instructed to dress for rain and wear old clothes under rain gear. In each cabin, one staff member conducts an activity. Use your imagination for this. Games like "Killer," "Charades," simulation games, crafts, movies, singing, etc. are all possibilities. Every 40 minutes or so, each group rotates to a new cabin, and a new activity. The leaders stay put with the same activity for the new group. This can continue until each group has experienced each activity. It really helps prevent boredom on those dreary days. (Contributed by Louie Vesser, Sweetwater, Tennessee)

WAGON TRAIN

Here's a new twist to an old idea, great as a different kind of camping experience.   Secure the use of an open field and enlist several truck or trailer campers or motorhomes. Park them in a circle. Have a campfire within the circle. With plenty of food, hot chocolate, games, singing, and spiritual thought, this makes a great overnight retreat. (Contributed by Danny Dye, Huntington Beach, California)

YOUR LOVING OFFSPRING

Most kids don't bother to "write home" while at summer camp, so here's a solution to that problem. Print up the following "letter" (or a similar one that you can create) and have the kids (all of them) fill it out. Provide envelopes and postage, and mail them out early in the week. Parents do enjoy hearing from their kids, and this is a fun way to get it done.

LETTER FROM CAMP *(circle the best answer.)*

Dear (a) folks (b) Sir (c) Ms. (d) Mommy and daddy (e)_____:

I am feeling (a) miserable (b) hungry (c) despondent (d) great (e) so-so (f) sick (g) lower than a snake's belly (h) as well as can be expected after breaking my leg (i)_____.

My financial condition is (a) zero (b) fine after I ripped off my counselor's wallet (c) okay (d) dependent on how fast you can send me some bread (e) I'm loaded (f)_____.

I will come home when (a) I run out of money (b) I feel like it (c) the sun refuses to come up in the morning (d) you promise to be nice to my new pet rattlesnake (e)_____.

I sleep a lot here because (a) I'm lazy (b) I like to save wear and tear on my clothes (c) I'm into energy conservation (d) my counselor keeps giving me some funny little pills (e)_____.

My spiritual life is (a) angelic (b) satanic (c) great (d) at low ebb (e) up and down (f)_____.

Most of my friends here are (a) boys (b) girls (c) squirrels (d) in trouble since they met me (e) not too bright (f) fine (g)_____.

Camp food is (a) rotten (b) okay (c) great (d) rationed (e) no nutritional value (f) fine, if you have an iron stomach (g)_____.

Yesterday I learned that (a) 2 and 2 make 4 (b) they'll send me home if I don't shape up (c) you moved (d) there's no such thing as Santa Claus (e) it hurts when you fall from a 50 foot high cliff (f)_____.

I have decided (a) to get married while I'm up here (b) that camps are for the birds (c) to join a rock and roll band (d)_____.

There isn't much else to say except: _____

Your loving offspring

_____
(signed)

(Contributed by Bill Vestal, Forest Park, Georgia)

Chapter Seven

Service Projects

CHRISTMAS LOCK-IN

If you are looking for a significant and meaningful activity for your youth group (ninth grade and above), the Christmas Lock-in is it. The Christmas Lock-in is a 36 hour event that is held one week before Christmas on a Friday and Saturday. Here is the schedule:

Friday

7:00 p.m. Contemporary Worship Service - run entirely by the kids focusing on the practical meaning of Christmas.
8:00 p.m. Free time for socializing.
9:00 p.m. Doors locked and work begins. Begin by making favors for the nursing home that the kids will be visiting Saturday. Then wrap gifts for poor families and the children at Children's Hospital (or the children's ward of any hospital). After that, pack food baskets for the poor (get the food from a congregational door collection along with funds raised from the youth themselves). The food that is purchased for the food baskets is bought during a midnight shopping spree.
After midnight: The kids sleep in the church.

Saturday

8:00 a.m. Breakfast.
9:00 a.m. Deliver baskets to the poor.
11:30 a.m. Lunch.
1:00 p.m. Carol singing and favors given out at nursing home.
3:00 p.m. Carol singing and gifts distributed at Children's Hospital.
6:00 p.m. Dinner.
7:00 p.m. Caroling to church members' homes.
9:00 p.m. Gala Christmas party with lots of singing, fellowship, and close with communion.

(Contributed by Douglas Janetzke, Roseville, Michigan)

CHRISTMAS TREE OF LOVE

At Christmas time, put a Christmas tree (either real or artificial) in the church foyer. Place a few decorations on the tree, but leave it embarrassingly bare. Leave a package of ornament hangers under the tree, along with a donation box, decorated to look like a gift. Ask the people of the church to consider hanging one of their Christmas cards on the tree with greetings to the entire congregation as an alternative to sending out individual cards to everyone The card can be hung on the tree by using one of the ornament hangers provided. Also ask them to donate the money that would be saved by not buying so many cards and by not paying so much postage to whatever worthy project you happen to have. The money can be deposited in the gift box under the tree. Of course, people can give more than the money they save if they choose.

People are generally more responsive to this if you have a specific project in mind, such as a missionary project, providing toys or other gifts for an orphanage, giving to a hunger relief agency, etc. Be sure to stress that this project is optional. If people would rather send personal greeting cards, they should be encouraged to do so. (Contributed by Larry D. Spicer, Great Falls, Montana)

DOMINO DROP

By now, we have all seen the incredible domino mazes in which dominoes are placed end to end in a huge design. Then the domino at the beginning of the design is pushed over and one by one the others fall until all the dominoes have fallen. Many of these designs are so intricate that it takes many minutes for all the dominoes to fall.

Have your youth group get people to pledge a certain amount of money per domino. Then have your group design a pattern of dominoes that will include as many dominoes as they can get their hands on. (They, of course, can practice ahead of time to find the best design possible.) When they have finished their final design of dominoes, they push the first one and watch them all fall. All of the fallen dominoes are counted and then multiplied times the pledge for each domino. This can be a great fund raiser and a lot of fun for everyone involved. (Contributed by Bob Moyer, Washington, Pennsylvania)

GLEANING PARTY

If your community has public garden plots or is in an area where there are many farms, your group might consider the old custom of gleaning. Going through the fields after the harvest and salvaging that which is ripe and usable. The food which is collected is sorted and then given to an organization which distributes food to the poor. (Contributed by Jim Couser, Downers Grove, Illinois)

GOLF CLUB WASH

Here's an unique fund raiser that gets good results. Set up a booth at the 18th green of a local golf course and offer to wash golf clubs for the tired hackers. All you need is permission from the golf course pro (or park board for municipal courses), a pail of soapy water, a brush, a pail of clean water, a coin collector, and a few towels. For extra service, you may want to wax the woods and use a metal polish on the irons. If the money is going to a worthy cause, most golfers will be glad to pay a reasonable price. (Contributed by Warren Ueckert, Peoria, Illinois)

H.O.P. CLUB

H.O.P. stands for "Help Older People" and the H.O.P. Club is a program in which teens and adults work together to assist the elderly with work that they are unable to do for themselves. This should be an on-going ministry as opposed to a one-shot service project type of thing. Skilled adults train the youth to do carpentry, plumbing, wiring, upholstery, or whatever needs to be done, and give direction and supervision while on the job. Younger kids can be involved in such tasks as washing windows and walls, raking leaves, shoveling snow, moving furniture, writing letters, and so on. Many other people who want to be involved, but less directly, can provide financial assistance, etc. The important thing is that it should be well organized, and carried out on a regular basis. Many senior citizens' groups can provide information on where the greatest needs are, and the elderly community can be informed that this service is available at no charge, or at a very low cost, to them.

A program such as this not only provides valuable relief for the elderly who must pay to have this work done, but also gives kids the opportunity to give of themselves in a meaningful way and to build relationships with a segment of society that they often ignore. (Contributed by Terry Stoops, Glenshaw, Pennsylvania)

KIDNAP THE PASTOR

Have the group "kidnap" the pastor or someone else well-known in the church (prearranged, of course!) with the ransom being an amount of canned goods (e.g. 100 cans) from the congregation to be used for distribution to needy families. This should be done on a Saturday. Kids then telephone people in the congregation inform- ing them of the kidnapping and the ransom. The collection can be made on Sunday morning. If the ransom isn't paid up, the youth can be prepared to handle the morning service or the responsibilities of the kidnapped person. (Contributed by Geoffrey Koglin, Des Moines, Iowa)

M.O.P. TEAMS

M.O.P. stands for "Missionary Orientation Program." The idea is to send young people off to mission fields to work with missionaries for a period of time, and to experience first hand what the mission field is like. M.O.P. carries a dual meaning, because it also tells people that the kids will actually mop floors in order to make enough money to make the trip. Most missionaries are happy to have enthusiastic young people come and help out with various projects for almost any period of time. A program such as this is often the turning point in a young person's life as they attempt to decide just how they want to serve God. (Contributed by Earl Justice, Jackson, Mississsippi)

PARTY MAKING PARTY

This is a great idea for youth groups that are tired of having parties and tired of helping others. . Have your youth groups put on a party for those groups you want to help. You could have a Sweetheart's Banquet for an old folks home, or the elderly in your congregation; or an Easter Egg Hunt for an orphanage or special education group; or a Christmas party for underprivileged kids; a Thanksgiving Banquet for underprivileged kids, widows, or college students who are away from home. (Contributed by Stephen Douglas Williford, Memphis, Tennessee)

PENNY DRIVE

The penny drive is a fund raiser that encourages maximum involvement from both your youth group and congregation and the rewards are worth it. A lot of money can be raised and very worthwhile projects can be accomplished with just pennies.

Get your senior high group to set a date and advertise only to the congregation. The project should be a one day event from 9 in the morning to 5 in the evening. Choose a mission project where the money is to be given and then develop themes and advertising that will be catchy and appealing to all in the church. ("Windmills for Ethiopia" or "Kilowatts for Katpadi", for example.)

People are notified in advance that the pennies are to be brought to the church on the specified day only. When people bring their pennies, have your youth group there to take the pennies and place them on a large picture cut out of white paper, which should be placed on the floor. As the pennies are placed on the picture, an effective mosaic-like design begins to form. People will come back all day long to watch how the design is progressing.

If people come with checks or dollar bills, have pennies on hand for exchange. (Simply go to a bank for a supply.) Once this event becomes a tradition, people will start saving pennies all year long in anticipation of the penny drive. (Contributed by Dick Vriesman, Holland, Michigan)

POST OFFICE

Here's a seasonal activity for young people to raise money for a Christmas project. Set up a "church post office" to beat inflation and to beat the slow mail service. It can be fancy or just a table. The church members drop their letters to be delivered as they come into the church. They pay either what they would in postage or just give a donation to the "postmaster." The young people sort the mail and give it out to the correct people as they come by to pick up any cards for them. For a good service project, the young people can deliver to the shut-ins and to people that don't come. You might start a "singing telegram" service and have a set fee for it. The money can be used for special Christmas projects or offerings. Once this starts, the church members will be looking for it every Christmas. Seems that more good will is shared within the church body. More people send cards when they know the money is going toward a good cause. (Contributed by Dave Gilliam, Grove, Oklahoma)

PINS FOR MISSIONS

Here's a fund raiser that has been done with great success. Secure the use of a bowling alley and set up a bowling tournament or just an evening of bowling with your young people. The object is to raise money for a worthy cause, which is done by taking pledges from adults and businessmen in the community. Each kid enlists the help of "sponsors" who pledge a certain amount of money (5 cents, 10 cents, 25 cents, or more) for each point scored while bowling. Each kid bowls three games and the total of the points scored in the three games is the number that determines the amount of each sponsor's pledge. In a tournament, the "winners" continue scoring more points, therefore collecting more money for the cause. One group called the event "Pins for Missions" and the money was used for world missions. (Contributed by David Peters, Florissant, Missouri)

SENSITIZING ACTIVITIES

Interacting with children who are retarded or have cerebral palsy cystic fibrosis, MS, or leukemia can be a uniquely moving and growing opportunity for kids. Have the youth group plan an on-going social activity for a group of such young people. Once a month plan some kind of activity (swimming, movie, field trips, play, camping) and include food, refreshments, etc. Of course, there must be close cooperation with the clinic or agency from which the contact is made. Such activities would have to be prefaced by a series of introductory meetings with qualified workers who could prepare your kids for the special do's and don'ts of working with that particular handicap. Some churches have formed ecumenical counsels and rotate the monthly activities among different youth groups. (Contributed by Dodd Lamberton, Minneapolis, Minnesota)

STAY AT HOME WORK CAMP

The idea of a work camp is not new, of course, but for many youth groups they simply do not have the resources for the travel and expense required by projects a long way from home. The Stay-At-Home Work Camp combines all the benefits of a work camp without leaving home.

Find a place a few miles out of town where your group can sleep and eat during the whole period of the work camp. (4 to 7 days.) The work projects themselves are determined by the needs of your own area and can include painting, remodeling, building buildings owned by those on fixed incomes such as elderly, widows, or those without income.

Whatever the project, the youth should raise the money for whatever expenses are involved for materials. You could also have members of the church buy "scholarships" to pay the room and board of each work camper.

To liven up the conference you can plan activities during the evening for the kids themselves like movies, game nights, etc. Also, if you take slides or super 8 films of the kids working, it makes for quite a program combined with testimonies from the group. (Contributed by Jim Beal, Newport, Arizona)

SUMMER CAROLING

One method of bringing joy to people who are sick or shut-in is a summer caroling experience. Youths visit homes to sing songs and perhaps even prepare meals to eat with the residents. This can be incorporated into "slave day" too, and work can be done for the needy. The minister might agree to join with the youth group and administer communion in the homes of people unable to attend church. Cassette tapes and recorders may be taken to bring worship services and messages from friends to those who cannot leave their homes. (Contributed by Denise Turner, Lima, Ohio)

TOY COLLECTION

Every town has some organization which collects toys at Christmas for needy children. A good group activity would be to have a toy drive, where the kids go door-to-door to collect old unwanted toys that are still usable, or that require minor repairs. They can be repaired, if necessary, and then distributed or given to an agency who distributes them. This can be made into a contest in which teams see who can collect the most toys within a given time limit. (Contributed by Jim Berkley, Ventura, California)

TREATS MAKING PARTY

Have your youth group spend an evening making popcorn balls, fudge cookies, and other treats. Then on Halloween, have them deliver the treats to an orphanage, hospital, or rest home. (Contributed by Corinne Bergstrom, Berthoud, Colorado)

Chapter Eight

Publicity & Promotion

FITNESS CALENDAR

Here is a mailer idea that combines some truth with absurdity and is a lot of fun:

Your Weekly FITNESS CALENDAR

MONDAY

Physical: Eat a bowl of Apple Jacks and sliced broccoli.
Social: Tell three of your friends that you really appreciate them.
Mental: Diagram the third law of Thermodynamics.
Spiritual: Thank God for all His good gifts and pray for peace.

TUESDAY

Physical: Do 100 push-ups and then arm wrestle Andy Granatelli.
Social: Throw a party for your entire student body.
Mental: Memorize the city charter and by-laws of Cleveland, Tennessee.
Spiritual: Thank God for His Word and pray for one friend who needs Jesus.

WEDNESDAY

Physical: Eat 7 rutabagas and jog to Port Hueneme and back.
Social: Spray your mouth with Desenex and wash your feet in Listerine.
Mental: Read "War and Peace" twice - once forward and once backward.
Spiritual: Read I Corinthians 4 and 5; come to youth club at 7:00 p.m.

THURSDAY

Physical: Come to church softball game, 7:30 p.m.
Social: Use plenty of Right Guard or you might be Left Out.
Mental: Define the law of gravity in three Arabic dialects.
Spiritual: Read the book of James in a modern speech New Testament.

FRIDAY

Physical: Tear a telephone book in half.
Social: Buy your best friend a small gift and leave it on his doorstep anonymously.
Mental: Add up all the house numbers on your street on an abacus.
Spiritual: Pray for your family, your neighbors, and your church.

SATURDAY

Physical: Swim the English channel and then challenge Bobby Riggs to a tennis game.
Social: Invite a friend over for rabbit dinner and serve carrots and lettuce.
Mental: Look up the word "quachil" and write a 1000 word paper on it.
Spiritual: Read a few Psalms of praise and then write a Psalm of praise yourself.

SUNDAY

Physical: Ride a unicycle to church and offer someone a ride home.
Social: Tell someone that you are glad to see them, and mean it.
Mental: Ask your Sunday School teacher to explain the period of the Macabbees.
Spiritual: Get into the Spirit of the services, and let the Spirit get into you.

Your Youth Group Info Here!

(Contributed by Ed Stewart, Glendale, California)

SCOREBOARD MAILER

Dear Friends,

As a public service to you, your youth department is sending along the scores to this week's big games.

> **Union 76, Phillips 66**
> **Colgate 100, NP 27**
> **Boeing 747, Indianapolis 500**
> **Brasil 77, Chicago 7**
> **Fairlane 500, Datsun 280**
> **US 101, Route 66**
> **Musketeers 3, Stooges 3 (tie)**
> **Spirit 76, Colt 45**

You will really know the score if you join in on all the activities listed below. We'll be looking for you!

(Your youth schedule listed here.)

(Contributed by Ed Stewart, Glendale, California

Chapter Nine

Special Section:
The Family

FAMILY CLUSTERS

If you would like to bring change to your normal Daily Vacation Bible School program, introduce the concept of Family Clusters. Invite the entire congregation (adults and children alike) to the church for a five consecutive night program. Divide the total group into small clusters of eight to ten members each. Instruct families to stay together. Your clusters will probably consist of a couple of four-member families and a couple of singles, or a family of five, a young married couple with no children, and two older adults. And that's exactly what you want. Nuclear families aligned with some "outsiders" forming new family clusters.

To begin the cluster activity, present a Task Card to each cluster. Design the Task Cards to help a cluster learn the subject of the Scripture being studied for the evening. For instance, if your subject is "Trusting the Lord in All Your Ways," you might have a Task Card instructing the clusters to try the Trust Circle. In the Trust Circle, the cluster sits in a tightly knit circle, legs inward. Then one person stands in the middle of the circle and falls. He or she is caught, of course, by the members of the cluster and is pushed to another part of the circle, falling and being caught. Or you could put on the Task Card a "Trust Walk" experience where one person with eyes open leads the rest of the cluster on a walk. Members of the cluster hold hands single file with their eyes shut. They are forced to trust the leader for their safety and their learning.

You'll probably discover that not only do people learn concepts during the nightly activities, but that family leaders learn how to lead activities. And this ability is then used by fathers and mothers in family experiences during the rest of the year.

ADULT-TEEN GAP CLASS

Once a year, invite adults and teenagers in the church to participate in an eight week, Wednesday night class. Invite any adult in the church whether or not they have teenagers living at home. And invite any teenager to come whether or not he or she is accompanied by a parent. Stress the activity- centered learning approach to maximize the group experience. Take various ideas from IDEAS books and activities from other curriculum aids you've found helpful. But avoid the lecture method like the plague. It's very hard to find a speaker who relates well to both adults and teens. Use role plays often. Even encourage role reversal where adults play the role of young people and vice versa. Focus on one concept a night throughout the eight weeks. You might want to work on such concepts as Trust, Listening, Love, etc. Design your class to facilitate communication and develop feelings of trust and communication between the two age groups.

On the last night, throw a party (an ice cream feed or hot dog roast). Give some time for members of the class to share what's happened in their lives and their outlook because of the class.

FAMILY FILM NIGHT

Sponsor a film night for families once a month. Borrow from the public library a Disney film or a set of Laurel and Hardy or Abbott and Costello shorts (most public libraries lend them free of charge, but reserve what you want well in advance) and invite families to come. Encourage parents to bring their children along with popcorn, pop, or whatever they want to eat during the film.

If your public library doesn't have what you want, check with various film outlets. You can usually rent Disney films and other family-oriented films for a nominal amount. If you do rent, charge each family a small sum to help subsidize the film.

If your junior high or senior high group needs to raise some funds, have them sell homemade goodies at the film night as well.

FAMILY NEWSLETTER

Instead of using church bulletin or church paper to announce family-related events, you might consider sending a monthly newsletter to all family units of the church. (A family unit consists of any type of living unit a church member is in- nuclear family unit, single parent home, grandparents' home, singles living unit, etc.)

To be most effective, write the letter in an informal, first person manner. In addition to announcements concerning family activities, include such items as: resources for family growth and family devotions, a list of television programs to watch or avoid during the month, questions for family discussions, and thoughts on family finances, managing a household, etc. Share ways you've grown through your own family as well. Also include information on what the church and community are doing for family units.

SENIOR HIGH MARRIAGE COURSE

Lead a course designed primarily for high school seniors on marriage. Make it much more than a sex education course. Instead, divide your group into "imaginary" couples. Marry each couple in a mock wedding ceremony. Then give them a hypothetical income and ask them to build a budget and then go out into the community and attempt to live on that budget. ("Going out into the community and living" is hypothetical, of course. Instruct them to simply go into stores and price what they'd like to buy from their budget. And then have them come back and report.) In the process of the course (which you should design to last several weeks, once a week), have each couple spin the "wheel of chance" several times. Design a spinner so that a couple has a chance to land on such items as "you've just found out you're pregnant", "your three year old son has cancer", "your house burned down", "you've been offered a job in Alaska" etc. After spinning the wheel, each couple has to discuss how they'll deal with this trauma emotionally, spiritually, and financially. Will they have to borrow money? Where will they have to go to borrow it? Who can they go to for counseling? Etc.

Design your course so that young people can come face to face in a simulated manner with the traumas involved in marriage before they're actually involved in this hallowed institution. And help them realize that it's important to have it together personally before they get married because people don't get it together by getting married.

FAMILY SEED CENTER

You can aid the families in your church by developing a "Family Seed Center." All you need is a bulletin board, a table, and the ability to find resources and events that pertain to the families in your congregation. Place on the bulletin board items that advertise church-sponsored or community-sponsored events that relate to families. Put on the board a list of television programs families might profit from watching together during the week. Put pictures of families in your church on the board. It's an excellent way to introduce families to one another in the church.

On the table, put any books or written resources you have on the family. You may want to begin to build a FAMILY LIFE LIBRARY by buying books on a regular basis that relate to family development. On the table, also include copies of your newsletters (if you decide to publish one) and any magazine articles that relate to the home. Each week, add new items to the table and the board so that people will gravitate to the center. Find a good location for the center as well. The foyer of the church or Christian education area of your church are two good spots. Analyze the traffic flow of your congregation and put the center where the people are.

A NOTE ON FAMILY MINISTRY

Don't try to do too much too soon. Family ministry is an evolving ministry and you'll find it's impossible to dump all these ideas on a church all at once. But you could begin gradually with I) Family Seed Center, or 2) a Family Night for the church, (Rent a YMCA gym and play games as a church family), or 3) a Family Emphasis Week at the church with guest speakers and activities for the whole family.

And if you decide to spend more time with families, begin to build a personal resource library. Read book reviews, browse through bookstores, and build a resource center that will be helpful to you and to the families you serve. (Contributed by Ron Rose, San Martin, California; edited by Denny Rydberg)